June 1995

Dear Stephanie –

... yet another milestone
in life – congratulations!

May you always know
of God's presence, guidance
and love –

wishing you peace –

Janice West

The Presbyterian Church of Okemos

WHAT ABOUT GOD?
NOW THAT YOU'RE
OFF TO COLLEGE

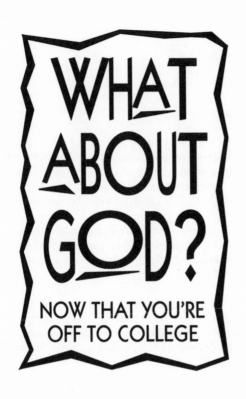

WHAT ABOUT GOD?

NOW THAT YOU'RE OFF TO COLLEGE

A PRAYER GUIDE

HELEN R. NEINAST
THOMAS C. ETTINGER

UPPER ROOM BOOKS
NASHVILLE

What About God?
Now That You're Off to College

The publisher gratefully acknowledges permission to reproduce the copyrighted material appearing in this book. Credit lines for this material appear on page 232 and following.

Scripture quotations not otherwise identified are from the New Revised Standard Version of the Bible, copyright 1989 by the Division of Christian Education of the National Council of the Churches of Christ in the United States of America, and are used by permission.

Scripture quotations designated RSV are from the Revised Standard Version of the Bible, copyright 1946, 1952, and © 1971 by the Division of Christian Education, National Council of the Churches of Christ in the United States of America, and are used by permission.

Cover design: Susan Scruggs
First Printing: March 1992 (10)
ISBN 0-8358-0655-3
Library of Congress Catalog Card Number: 91-67171

Printed in the United States of America

CONTENTS

INTRODUCTION   13

June / Week One   23
WORDS TO THE ALREADY WISE:
    What We Wish We'd Known at Age 18
June / Week Two   27
VOCATIONS, CAREERS, AND CALLINGS:
    Thoughts for Summer Reflection
June / Week Three   33
BY WHAT NAME WILL YOU BE CALLED?
    Wrestling with Your Identity
June / Week Four   37
UNDERSTANDING GOD'S WILL FOR YOUR LIFE
July / Week One   41
THE PRACTICE OF PRAYER
July / Week Two   45
PRACTICING PRAYER: *On Your Knees*
July / Week Three   49
PRACTICING PRAYER:*On the Run*
July / Week Four   53
PRACTICING PRAYER: *On the Level*
August / Week One   57
CHOICE MAKING
August / Week Two   61
WHO IS GOD? *Doing Your Own Theology*
August / Week Three   67
STUDYING THE BIBLE:
    Finding Yourself in the Faith Story
August / Week Four   71
LEAVING HOME:
    What to Take Along, What to Leave Behind
September / Week One   77
CHANGE: *Finding Your Way in a New Place*
September / Week Two   83
LOVING GOD WITH YOUR MIND:

The Sacredness of Study
September | Week Three   87
THE HOLINESS OF TIME:
  Time Management from a Faith Perspective
September | Week Four   93
SHRINKING EXPECTATIONS
October | Week One   97
LIFE IN THE BALANCE
October | Week Two   101
LIFE IN THE BALANCE: *Love and Relationships*
October | Week Three   105
LIFE IN THE BALANCE:
  The Refreshment of Play and Rest
October | Week Four   109
LIFE IN THE BALANCE: *Reaching Beyond Yourself*
November | Week One   113
SEXUALITY: *God's Amazing Gift*
November | Week Two   119
THE TYRANNY OF GRADES: *Measuring Yourself*
November | Week Three   123
TROUBLE, TEMPTATION, AND OTHER TRYING TIMES
November | Week Four   129
THE POWER OF GRATITUDE
December | Week One   133
FINDING GOD IN SOLITUDE AND QUIET
December | Week Two   137
FINDING GOD AMID THE NOISE AND PRESSURE
December | Week Three   141
PEACEMAKING IN A VIOLENT WORLD
December | Week Four   145
GOD WITH US: *The Gift of the Incarnation*
January | Week One   149
CLEARING THE SLATE: *The Gift of Forgiveness*
January | Week Two   153
LOVING YOURSELF AS GOD LOVES YOU
January | Week Three   157
SUCCESS AND FAILURE

January / Week Four   161
HARD TIMES: *Mourning and Being Comforted*

February / Week One   165
GOD'S EXTRAVAGANT GRACE:
    Surrounding You in Love

February / Week Two   169
GOD'S EXTRAVAGANT GRACE:
    Making Your Brokenness Whole

February / Week Three   173
GOD'S EXTRAVAGANT GRACE:
    Smoothing Out the Rough Edges

February / Week Four   177
ANGER, FEAR, AND GUILT: *The Unholy Trinity*

March / Week One   181
REFLECTIONS ON FAITH

March / Week Two   185
REFLECTIONS ON HOPE

March / Week Three   189
REFLECTIONS ON LOVE

March / Week Four   193
BLESSED TO BE A BLESSING:
    Sacrifice and Servant Leadership

April / Week One   197
LAUGHTER: *Does God Have a Sense of Humor?*

April / Week Two   201
LOVE YOUR MOTHER: *You and the Planet*

April / Week Three   205
WINNERS AND LOSERS

April / Week Four   209
EMBRACING DOUBT

May / Week One   213
THE RISKY BUSINESS OF TRUST

May / Week Two   217
LET GO AND LET GOD

May / Week Three   221
REFLECTING ON THE YEAR:
    Looking Backward, Looking Forward

May / Week Four   225
MOVING ON IN FAITH

REFLECTING ON THE MONTH: WEEK FIVE   231
ACKNOWLEDGMENTS   232
INDEX OF READINGS   237

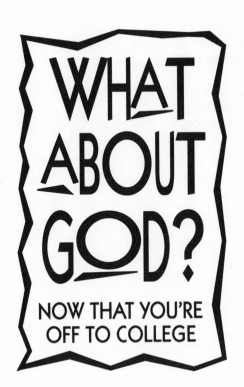

WHAT ABOUT GOD?

NOW THAT YOU'RE OFF TO COLLEGE

So . . . What About God Now That You're Out of High School?

You've made it through high school. Survived geometry, given your all for the team, worked a part-time job to put gas in the car, reported for the high school newspaper, partied through prom night, cheered the school on to victory, cut class once or twice, studied hard, and played even harder.

COLLEGE IS NEXT

So what's next with God?

God was there all through high school. At times you felt it more than at others, but there were moments when you knew for sure, deep down inside, that God was with you. Sure, there were plenty of times you doubted. But somehow that was OK, too.

But what about God now that you're off to college? Does God go to college with you or not?

College is a four-year-long series of opportunities, crises, and adventures. (More adventure than crisis, probably.) New people, places, and things. Choosing a major. Funding your studies. Facing that first college exam.

Exploring relationships and rearranging the way you feel about yourself. Living in a dorm or off campus on your own. Growing up in totally new and amazing and frightening ways.

Your relationship with God will probably change, too. The God your parents and your minister and your youth group counselor taught you about is alive and well and traveling to college with you. In fact, God is already at college, anxiously awaiting your arrival.

GOD IS THERE

Sometimes you can feel that God is as far away as the home you left seven hundred miles and two weeks ago to come to college—or the home you leave each day for the commute to classes.

But God is there.

You just have to look. Maybe in some unexpected places. Maybe in some unexpected ways. And amid some pretty unexpected situations.

But God is there, searching for you even as you search for God.

This book can be a help to you in your search for a closer relationship with God over this next year. Amid all the challenges and changes that graduation from high school brings, this book is meant as a guide to a spiritual discipline of prayer and reflection that can be a touchstone, a lifeline, a way to grow in your relationship with God.

HOW TO USE THIS BOOK

This book contains material for daily prayer and reflection. It is organized around weekly themes, daily scripture readings, journal keeping, and personal prayer time.

Start each month's readings on the first Sunday of that month. For instance, if the first day of June is a Friday, start June's reflection on Sunday, June 3. If there are a couple of days left in the month after you've finished the four weeks of readings, use the page titled "Reflecting on the Month," page 231, to finish out the time until the next month's first Sunday.

Opening Prayer and Scripture Focus. Each week's reflection begins with a prayer calling you into God's presence and asking God to come into your presence. There is also a scripture that will be the focus for the week. We, the authors, have found the Scripture Focus for the week to be very important in our lives. In many cases, we have memorized these verses as part of our own spiritual discipline. You may find yourself doing the same.

To begin your time apart with God, pray the Opening Prayer. Read the Scripture Focus to yourself, either silently or aloud. Give yourself a few moments of silence, or stillness, to let the prayer and the scripture quiet your mind and heart. Allow yourself to be opened to hear what God has to say to you.

Daily Scripture Readings. Daily Scripture Readings are chosen each day to add to and expand on the theme for reflection each week.

We see the Bible as being our best source for knowledge about God and about the faith community. Scripture, tradition, reason, and experience each give us important information about who God is and who God intends us to be.

Many times the Daily Scripture Readings will include parts of the Psalms, the Gospels, the letters of Paul, the writings of the prophets, or the teachings of Moses. Find a translation of the Bible that speaks to you. The scriptures are a dynamic collection of writings, and there are several translations that seek to be both true to the original texts and readable for Christians today.

As you read each day's scripture, ask yourself several questions. How does the scripture apply to the week's Focus for Reflection? How does it apply to your life? to current events? What words of comfort does the scripture speak to you? What words of challenge? Open yourself to the scripture readings, and they will open themselves to you.

Focus for Reflection. After the Opening Prayer, Scripture Focus, and Daily Scripture Reading, the Focus for Reflection is introduced. The theme may be related to a specific issue in your life—leaving home, choosing a vocation, dealing with the pressures of academics—or it may focus on some aspect of your spiritual life— gratitude, grace, the sacredness of time.

Read the Focus for Reflection. As you read it, make note of any feelings or questions the piece raises for you.

Points of Departure. Following the Focus for Reflection are a few writings collected from various sources. Use these as points of departure for your reflection on the week's theme. One of them may speak to you more strongly than the others. Read them each day, and let yourself be guided to the one (or more) that calls to you.

Because we are sensitive to inclusive language about people (not using *he* when the object referred to is *he* or *she*) and inclusive images for God, we have changed male generic language to inclusive language wherever possible. In places where copyright holders did not give us permission to make changes, we left the original wording. As you read these, keep in mind that these authors were often writing without an understanding of our more recent notions about inclusive language.

Journaling: Ideas for Written Reflection. A journal can be one of the most important tools for faith exploration. Maybe you're in the habit of keeping a journal for yourself. Maybe you're not. Maybe you've kept a journal some time in the past, but don't any longer.

Now is a good time to begin, or to continue, journal keeping. In *Keeping a Spiritual Journal*, Harry Cargas and Roger Radley note that "a journal is a book in which you keep a record of events in your life, of your different relationships, of your response to things, of your feelings about things—of your search to find out who you are and what the meaning of your life might be. It is a book in which you carry out the greatest of life's adventures—the discovery of yourself."

Buy yourself a notebook—an inexpensive one from the college bookstore. Use the journal suggestions for the week to reflect on whatever your prayer and your study of the scriptures and the readings have brought out for you. Record your feelings, your fears, and your doubts, as well as new insights, images, and learnings that come to you.

This journal, unlike some you may have kept for school or other projects before, is strictly for you. Be as honest as you can in your journal— both with yourself and with God. Write for yourself—not for anyone else.

Try to write every day. Some days you may write only a sentence or two. Other days, you may fill a page or more. The important thing is to keep writing. God speaks powerfully through journal keeping. This discipline is a real gift of the spiritual life.

Keeping a journal also gives you a record of where you have been and where you are going in your spiritual life. Your journal will give you the chance to look back over the past days, weeks, and months to discover how your thoughts, feelings, and faith have changed over time.

Prayers. After you have finished your journal writing, take a few moments to center down for prayer. You might want to make a list at the end of your journal entry of people and circumstances you wish to lift before God in prayer. Spend time in the quietness, talking to God and listening to God.

You may find it easy to express gratitude and to ask for God's intercession in your prayers. These are important. Remember, though, to share honestly on all levels with God in your prayers. Be willing to bring all your feelings, your doubts, and your misgivings to God in prayer.

In *A Guide to Prayer for All God's People*, Rueben Job and Norman Shawchuck write that there are two conditions important "to nurture a consistent prayer discipline, solitude and silence. Solitude is being by oneself. Silence is the quality of stillness within and around oneself." They suggest selecting one time and place for prayer where you can go daily. "You will soon," they say, "find God is waiting for you in that place."

WHEN, WHERE, AND HOW: FINDING THE RIGHT TIME AND PLACE

Finding the right time and place for your prayer and meditation is a very personal thing. Some people function best in the mornings; others find their quiet centered time at the end of the day. It may take you a while to discover what time works best for you. Experiment until something feels right.

Whether you choose morning, noon, or the close of the day, the important thing is to develop a pattern, some regular time and place set aside for daily prayer and meditation. Choose a quiet place and a time with relatively few distractions. Then, keep your appointment with God at that time and in that place.

Some people find that lighting a candle or sitting quietly for a few moments and breathing deeply helps to focus their prayer time. Listen to your own inner spirit, and let yourself be guided to what you need to begin and end your quiet time with God.

What if you miss a day? Who cares! Don't be compulsive about it, and don't berate yourself. God wants you to grow in grace, not set yourself up for failure or harsh criticism. The spiritual life is one of gradual growth, not perfectionism. God does not expect perfection from you—maybe you shouldn't expect it from yourself, either.

THE CHURCH YEAR VERSUS THE ACADEMIC YEAR

It's odd, but there's a certain tension between the church's calendar of beginnings and endings and the way the academic year marks time. School gears up in the midst of Pentecost, a time the faith community calls "ordinary time"— though it by no means will be ordinary for you this fall.

Then, just as the school year is heading into the mad rush of finals, that watershed marking the end of your first semester in college, the church calendar asks you to slow down, to wait and watch during Advent, the beginning of the Christian year.

And, while the rest of the world is celebrating Christmas, you may find yourself collapsing in exhaustion as finals are, finally, finished.

Second semester has its own idiosyncrasies, the most obvious being spring break and Holy Week/Easter. Sometimes they coincide and you're faced with the challenge of keeping Holy Week holy in the middle of the one break you have to let off steam from school. Other times, Holy Week will fall during just another week of classes and work. It can be confusing.

Our best advice is to take some extra time during these holy days of the Christian year, to focus, to center, to remind yourself of your grounding in the faith. School—whether it's finals or spring break—will be the richer for it.

SO . . . WHAT ABOUT IT?

So . . . what *about* God now that you're out of high school? Lots of things will change for you in this next year—even your relationship with God.

We encourage you to take on the challenge of a daily walk with God in the year ahead.

Sometimes the journey will be full of high adventure, insight, and energy. Other times it may be dull and boring—a matter of going through the motions. Stay with it. You'll be amazed at the power and wonders God can work in your life if you stay open to God, week by week, one day at a time.

WORDS TO THE ALREADY WISE:
What We Wish We'd Known at Age 18

Opening Prayer

Supporting God, help me as I seek to stay open to growth. May your grace keep urging me to grow toward you and your perfect love. Amen.

Scripture Focus

For the Lord gives wisdom. (Proverbs 2:6)

Daily Scripture Readings

Sunday	Luke 6:46-49
Monday	Proverbs 2:1-11
Tuesday	Psalm 119:33-35
Wednesday	2 Chronicles 9:1-9
Thursday	Matthew 25:1-13
Friday	Psalm 1:1-3
Saturday	Luke 2:52

The Focus for Reflection

You are no doubt getting lots of advice as you graduate from high school and head off to college. That seems to be the way people—those who love you as well as those who don't even know you—deal with life's major transitions. They give advice.

"Keep your socks and your nose clean." That was my mother's favorite advice. "Be careful. Have fun. Don't do anything I wouldn't do." That was my dad's favorite.

An essay writer in *Time* magazine a few years back advised his high school graduate daughter to be herself—unless she discovered that her self was not who she wanted to be. In that case, the writer-father said, "Be someone else."

Some commencement addresses talk about defining success, striving for success, dealing with success. Other commencement addresses—the really good ones—also mention failure and other human frailties.

In these pages you won't read a lot of counsel about going to church or keeping your faith active or taking time to stay centered by developing a strong prayer life—though all of that is good advice. Waiting for you in Points of Departure are gleanings from the writings and thoughts of women and men who have something important, succinct, and provocative to say to you.

Sydney J. Harris, a newspaper columnist who wrote about everything from global war to marriage and family to the life of the spirit, called what he had to say "What I Wish I Had Known at Eighteen." Read on. See if any of it rings true.

Oh, and don't forget to be yourself.

Points of Departure

Δ What I Wish I Had Known at Eighteen. . . .

—That we do not grow up *uniformly*, but in spots and streaks; so that we may be mentally mature but *still* emotionally underdeveloped, or have a good practical grasp but *still* lack spiritual depth. . . .

—That the way to persuade [people] is not to beckon [them] to come and look at things from where *you* stand, but to move over to where [*they*] stand and then try to walk hand in hand to where you would like both of you to stand.

—That the best (and, ultimately, the only) way to make a "good impression" is by *becoming who you are*, not by trying to conform to anyone else's standard of what you ought to be.

—From *For the Time Being* by Sydney J. Harris

Δ I would give [high school graduates] this list of things that grown-ups do:

—clean the sink strainer
—plunge out the toilet
—clean up babies when they poop and pee
—wipe runny noses . . .
—carry out the garbage . . .
—bury dead pets when they get run over in the street.

It can get even worse than the list suggests. My wife is a doctor, and I won't tell you what she tells me she has to do sometimes. . . .

A willingness to do your share of cleaning up the mess is a test. And taking out the garbage of this life is a condition of membership in community.

—From *It Was on Fire When I Lay Down on It* by Robert Fulghum

Δ Charles A. Beard, an American historian, was once asked by a student if he could sum up in five minutes everything he had learned in a half century of teaching and writing. Professor Beard said he could do better than that; he could sum up everything he had learned in four sentences:

1) The bee that robs the flower also fertilizes it.

2) When it is dark enough you can see the stars.

3) Whom the gods would destroy, they first make mad with power.

4) The mills of the gods grind slowly but they grind exceedingly well.

—From *Human Options* by Norman Cousins

Journaling: Ideas for Written Reflection

Identify a couple of areas—self-discipline, keeping a balance of rest and work, making your own decisions—in which you wish to grow over the next year. What wisdom do you already have in these areas? What do you need to become more wise about?

Prayers: For the World, for Others, for Myself

VOCATIONS, CAREERS, AND CALLINGS:
Thoughts for Summer Reflection

Opening Prayer

Loving God, you have made me in your image—gifted, special, unique. Guide me as I seek your way. Help me to hear your voice, calling me today. Amen.

Scripture Focus

You are the salt of the earth; . . . You are the light of the world. (Matthew 5:13-14)

Daily Scripture Readings

Sunday	Micah 6:8
Monday	Mark 1:16-20
Tuesday	1 Samuel 3:1-10
Wednesday	Amos 7:14-15
Thursday	Matthew 25:14-30
Friday	1 Corinthians 12:4-31
Saturday	1 Timothy 4:11-16

The Focus for Reflection

You've heard it said before. I know you have. It may have been your parents, your professors, or a Pepsi commercial, but I know you've heard it. You are the next generation. The next generation of leaders. The class of 1992 or 1993 or 1994 or 1995. You are on the leading edge, the forefront of history.

So you've heard it before. But this week, in your reflection, hear it all again, this time in a new way. You are the next generation. Hear it as a call from God; hear it as a call to find your vocation; hear it as a call to meet the world at its leading edge.

For you, this year and the next three ahead of it are a time to explore, to listen, to dream, to hear the call to vocation. These next weeks and months can be your call to awaken to who you are and what you are called to do.

The call to vocation is, for you, not unlike the call, the moment of decision for the Israelites as they stood at the edge of the Red Sea, hearing Moses' and Miriam's call to follow to the water's edge as it parted to beckon them on to the new Jerusalem.

The call to vocation is, for you, not unlike the call the disciples heard when Jesus said, "If any want to become my followers, let them deny themselves and take up their cross and follow me" (Matt. 16:24).

The call to vocation. It is at times wondrous, at times elusive, at times downright confusing.

As you struggle with your call to vocation, remember that Jesus also struggled with his. He had to discover who he was in relationship to God and what it was that God intended him to do. The Holy Spirit led him on his vocational quest.

At Jesus' baptism, the Holy Spirit revealed him to be the Son of God. Then, he was led into the wilderness to wrestle with what that identity meant in the work he was to do. Even after Jesus turned away from the temptations in the wilderness in order to follow his vocation, his calling was not always affirmed by the people of God. In Luke 4, after Jesus' first public speech in the temple, his hearers were "filled with rage." They rose up and ran him out of town.

Even at the last, Jesus struggled with his calling. His deep uncertainty at the garden of Gethsemane just before his betrayal and death reveals that, even then, he struggled to listen for God's call.

God has, in some way or another, called you to the place you are right here, right now, on the edge of your first year in college. May it be for you a holy place, a joyful place, a place to explore, to play, to risk, to act, and to grow.

May it be for you, most of all, a place to listen . . . to listen for the call of God. You never know what you might discover.

Points of Departure

Δ Because our gifts carry us out into the world and make us participants in life, the uncovering of them is one of the most important tasks confronting any one of us. When we talk about being true to ourselves—being the persons we are intended to be—we are talking about gifts. We cannot be ourselves unless we are true to our gifts. When we talk about vocation, whether we are artists or engineers, we are talking about gifts. . . .

Whenever we struggle with what we are to do in life, we are struggling to uncover our talent or gift. For many it is a lifetime struggle.
—From *Eighth Day of Creation* by Elizabeth O'Connor

Δ The place God calls you to is the place where your deep gladness and the world's deep hunger meet.
—From *Wishful Thinking* by Frederick Buechner

Δ God is hiding in the world. Our task is to let the divine emerge from our deeds.
—From *God in Search of Man* by Abraham Joshua Heschel

Δ Our vocation is not a sphinx's riddle, which we must solve in one guess or else perish.
—From *No Man Is an Island* by Thomas Merton

Δ Nothing feeds the center so much as creative work.
—From *Gift from the Sea* by Anne Morrow Lindbergh

Journaling: Ideas for Written Reflection
Sometimes you know clearly what you want to do, and you can set clear goals. Other times, you feel as though your sense of direction is lacking, and you keep hoping things will fall into place on their own. Where would you place yourself on a continuum of "a strong sense of purpose and goals" at one end to "a clear sense of uncertainty and lack of goals" at the other? How do you feel about where you placed yourself?

People hear God's call to vocation in a number of different ways—sometimes by considering what they like to do, sometimes by following the guidance of family or a professor or a close friend, sometimes by sitting quietly and listening for God's nudging. How do you experience the call of God in your life?

Prayers: For the World, for Others, for Myself

BY WHAT NAME WILL YOU BE CALLED?
Wrestling with Your Identity

Opening Prayer

O God of many names, keep me in your care this week; let me know that I am yours. Amen.

Scripture Focus

Behold, my covenant is with you . . . No longer shall your names be Abram [and Sarai], but Abraham and Sarah. (Genesis 17:4-5, paraphrase)

Daily Scripture Readings

Sunday	Genesis 32:13-32
Monday	Luke 15:11-24
Tuesday	Exodus 2:1-10
Wednesday	Mark 5:1-20
Thursday	Ephesians 3:14-19
Friday	Genesis 2:18-25
Saturday	John 1:19-23

The Focus for Reflection

"What's your major? Where are you from? Where'd you go to high school? Who's your roommate?"

During your first weeks at college, you'll likely be asked—and be asking—these questions over and over again. New people, new faces, new personalities to sort through.

It all comes down to this: Who are you? Who do you want to be?

College is your next opportunity to establish who you are, to try out a new identity, to change some basic things about yourself, to take off in a new direction. College is a four-year chance to push out beyond where you are now and to explore some new territory.

It all comes down to this: Who are you? Who do you want to be?

In the months ahead, these questions will sometimes beckon you—challenging and energizing you to dig deeper inside yourself for answers. Other times, these same questions will somehow intimidate you—frustrating and confusing you with the kinds of answers you find inside yourself.

For most of the people in the Bible, the faith journey was a journey of self-identity—Who am I? Who do I want to be? One person in particular comes to mind.

His name is Moses. Born a Hebrew, saved from Egyptian slaughter when his mother put him into the Nile River in a reed basket, found by Pharaoh's daughter, and raised in the royal household. A good set-up for a major identity crisis. Moses, knowing his Hebrew roots, watches his people's oppression and slavery, until one day he can stand it no longer, and he kills an Egyptian who had been beating a Hebrew slave. In that moment, and in the years to come, he hears a radically different answer to the question, "Who am I?"

Coming to understand who you are and who you want to be may at times seem like Moses' sudden act of self-discovery.

Moses might have given up his struggle and ignored his people's suffering. But he didn't. He kept asking the questions—Who am I? Who do I want to be?—until the answers began to come.

As you make your way along the journey of self-discovery, remember that Moses received a call from God to free the Hebrews.

In the process of finding out *who* you are, never forget *whose* you are: God's own daughter, God's own son.

Points of Departure

Δ It is a truism—and one of the annoying things about truisms is that they are true—that most of us spend a good deal of our lives coming to understand who we are.
—From *A Life to Live—A Way to Pray* by John B. Coburn

Δ Like Moses, we often feel the frustration and anger that come when we cannot decide on a path to follow. We can't fit into life lived before, yet the path before us is dark and uncertain. No wonder we feel like two different people, one choosing one path, the other deciding on another way.
—From *Healing Wisdom from the Bible* by James E. Gibson

Δ Look for yourself, and you will find in the long run only hatred, loneliness, despair, rage, ruin, and decay. But look for Christ and you will find Him, and with Him everything else thrown in.

—From *Mere Christianity* by C.S. Lewis

Journaling: Ideas for Written Reflection

What are some of the adjectives that could be used to describe you? If someone were describing you, what would you want him or her to say?

Prayers: For the World, for Others, for Myself

UNDERSTANDING GOD'S WILL FOR YOUR LIFE

Opening Prayer

May your Holy Spirit guide me, now and always, O God. Amen.

Scripture Focus

What does the Lord require of you but to do justice, and to love kindness, and to walk humbly with your God? (Micah 6:8)

Daily Scripture Readings

Sunday	Luke 2:13-14
Monday	Colossians 1:9-10
Tuesday	Luke 22:42
Wednesday	Proverbs 3:13-18
Thursday	Ephesians 1:11-14
Friday	Matthew 7:24-27
Saturday	John 3:16-17

The Focus for Reflection

"I've studied for this test all I'm going to. If I fail the course, it's God's will."

"He was so young. But God called him home. His death must be God's will."

"If I only knew God's will for my life, I could concentrate better on my studies."

Lots of things—good and bad—get attributed to God as God's will. It's tough sometimes to know when and how God is acting in the world.

And how do you tell when something is God's will and when it is just your own will? It's confusing.

Little Katie, a child in my church, was so alive, so full of energy before she got sick. A wonderful kid. Yet she contracted leukemia at the tender age of three. Why her? Why anyone?

As the illness progressed, it became impossible to count all those who joined in the fight to help Katie. I watched the hospital staff care so much—hating the pain of the treatments even as they inflicted them. I watched simple people, those whom Jesus called the salt of the earth, increase their saltiness even as they suffered along with Katie's family. They said prayers, expressed doubt, prayed in faith, hoped against hope, and loved unceasingly.

When I consider all that happened those three years, the calls, cards, food, donations, visits, and prayers on behalf of Katie, I know that I am closer to understanding God's will. It's like Harold Kushner says in *When Bad Things Happen to Good People:* The issue is not "where does the tragedy come from?" but "where does it lead?" God calls each of us to use our hearts, minds, souls, and strength to learn, to care, to love, and yes, to cure disease. God has already given us all we need to do these very things.

The battle against leukemia goes on. Yet this particular battle for Katie's life is over. She died in the fall of 1991 at the age of six. It is yet another mystery, this time a sad one.

God's will does make itself known—in the actions of people, in the words of the Bible, and through your own reason and experience. As you seek to do God's will—to love God with your whole being and to love your neighbor as yourself—you may not find answers to all your questions; but you will, day by day, learn to discern the will of God—both for your life and for the life of the world.

Points of Departure

Δ The question is not whether the things that happen to you are chance things or God's things because, of course, they are both at once. There is no chance thing through which God cannot speak—even the walk from the house to the garage that you have walked ten thousand times before, even the moments when you cannot believe there is a God who speaks at all anywhere. [God] speaks, I believe, and the words [God] speaks are incarnate in the flesh and blood of our selves and of our own footsore and sacred journeys.
—From *The Sacred Journey* by Frederick Buechner

Δ Unfortunately, many people view the will of God as rather like a ten-ton elephant hanging overhead, ready to fall on them. . . . Actually, the word which we translate into English as *will* comes from both a Hebrew and a Greek word which means "yearning." It is that yearning which lovers have for one another. Not a yearning of the mind alone or of the heart alone but of the *whole being*. A yearning which we feel is only a glimmering of the depth of the yearning of God for us.

—From *The Breath of Life* by Ron DelBene

Δ Do not hastily ascribe things to God. Do not easily suppose dreams, voices, impressions, visions, or revelations to be from God. They may be from [God]. They may be from nature. They may be from the devil.

—John Wesley

Journaling: Ideas for Written Reflection

How do you understand God's will for your life? Are there times when you experience clear guidance about some things and only vague directions about others?

Prayers: For the World, for Others, for Myself

THE PRACTICE OF PRAYER

Opening Prayer

May the words of my mouth and the meditations of my heart bring me closer to you, O wondrous Friend. Amen.

Scripture Focus

Then Jesus told them a parable about their need to pray always and not to lose heart. (Luke 18:1)

Daily Scripture Readings

Sunday	Luke 11:1-13
Monday	Exodus 33:7-11
Tuesday	Psalm 63:1-4
Wednesday	Luke 18:1-17
Thursday	2 Chronicles 30:21-27
Friday	Matthew 7:9-11
Saturday	Isaiah 56:6-8

The Focus for Reflection

Frederick Buechner says that everybody prays, whether they think of it as prayer or not. He believes that prayer makes itself known in all sorts of forms—the silence that comes when you confront something amazing and wonderful, the pain you feel when someone you love hurts, the angry cry when someone hurts you, the hope rising in your heart when you hear news that is too good *not* to be true.

Lots of people have written lots of books about the practice of prayer. Prayer as listening to God. Prayer as talking to God. Prayer as adoration, confession, thanksgiving, supplication. Prayer as the silence that comes with a deep peace. Prayer that cries out loud to God in anguish. Prayer that slowly, ever so slowly, changes the heart of the one who prays.

In the Bible, it seems that the most important thing about prayer is to keep at it. In Luke, Jesus tells two stories about the practice of prayer. In one, he says that prayer is like knocking on a friend's door at midnight to borrow bread—knocking and knocking until the sleepy friend finally gets up and gives you the bread you're asking for. In another, he says that the practice of prayer is like approaching the crooked judge who doesn't want to hear the poor widow's case, but finally does simply because of her persistence.

Whatever else prayer is—petition, confession, thanksgiving, or silence shared between you and God—the Bible says that prayer must be practiced over and over and over again. For it is in the practice of prayer that we seek God and God seeks us.

Practice prayer. Keep at it. No matter what. Even when the answers you get are not the ones you expected or prayed for, remember this—that prayer is beating a path to God's door, and allowing God to beat a path to yours.

Points of Departure

Δ The way to pray is to begin with yourself.
There is no other way. If you want to, you begin;
if you do not want to, no one can make you. . . .
    As on any journey, we have to start out just as
we are and from where we are. The only self who
can make this journey is the self we are at the
moment.
—From *A Life to Live—A Way to Pray* by John B. Coburn

Δ When I pray . . . I hold a silly, naive or deadly
serious dialogue with what is deepest inside me.
—From *An Interrupted Life* by Etty Hillesum

Δ Those of us who have come to make regular
use of prayer would no more do without it than
we would refuse air, food, or sunshine. And for
the same reason. When we refuse air, light, or
food, the body suffers. And when we turn away
from meditation and prayer, we likewise deprive
[ourselves] of . . . the light of God's reality, the
nourishment of [God's] strength, and the
atmosphere of [God's] grace.
—From *The Twelve Steps and Twelve Traditions of Alcoholics
Anonymous*

Δ It is always right to pray for healing. It is also
all right to pray for curing as long as we are
willing to accept that this may not be God's will,
as long as we are willing to accept God's will
rather than our own. Above the lintel of a church
in New England are carved these words:

REMEMBER, NO IS AN ANSWER.
—From *The Irrational Season* by Madeleine L'Engle

Δ Prayer does not change God, but it changes the one that offers it.
—Søren Kierkegaard

Δ All this reminds me of something I heard about the Hopi Indians. They don't think there is much difference between praying and dancing—that both are necessary for a long life. The Hopis should know, I guess, as they have been through a lot and are still around. They say that to be a useful Hopi is to be one who has a quiet heart and takes part in all the dances.
—From *It Was on Fire When I Lay Down on It* by Robert Fulghum

Journaling: Ideas for Written Reflection
Think about your own "practice of prayer." Do you have a pattern, a schedule, a regular time to "center down" and talk with God? Is the path between your door and God's well-traveled, or do you need more practice on that path?

Prayers: For the World, for Others, for Myself

PRACTICING PRAYER:
On Your Knees

Opening Prayer

Draw me close to you, O God, so that when I pray, I can hear even your whisper. Amen.

Scripture Focus

In the morning, while it was still very dark, [Jesus] got up and went out to a deserted place, and there he prayed. (Mark 1:35)

Daily Scripture Readings

Sunday	Daniel 6:10-11
Monday	1 John 1:8-9
Tuesday	Matthew 26:36-44
Wednesday	Deuteronomy 9:25-26
Thursday	Psalm 95:1-7
Friday	Matthew 6:5-13
Saturday	1 Samuel 1:24-28

The Focus for Reflection

Hannah, in the Old Testament, stood before God to pray when she dedicated her son Samuel to God's service. Ezra the scribe fell on his knees and spread his hands out to God to pray. The Book of Psalms records believers with their hands lifted up toward heaven in prayers of thanksgiving, or with their eyes downcast in prayers of sorrow or confession. When Jesus prayed in Gethsemane, he knelt by himself to pray to God.

The practice of prayer "on your knees" is not so much about your posture when you pray as it is about your approach when you pray.

Hannah, standing, was pouring out the deepest part of her heart to God. Ezra, kneeling with his hands spread out on the ground, was offering his deepest prayer to God. Believers with their hands uplifted or their eyes downcast were praying out of the depths of their faith. Jesus, kneeling in the garden of Gethsemane, was giving God the very center of his being, his innermost thoughts and feelings.

God invites you to bring the depths of yourself to prayer. When you are so full or so empty, so overwhelmed or so overjoyed, that you cannot pray, God promises that if you simply bring yourself to prayer, the Spirit will pray for you—whether you are standing on your feet or bowed down on your knees.

God promises to pray with you, for you, even when you cannot pray for yourself. All you have to do is give God the chance to be there for you—any time, any place, any posture.

Points of Departure

Δ For me, prayer is an upward leap of the heart, an untroubled glance towards heaven, a cry of gratitude and love which I utter from the depths of sorrow as well as from the heights of joy.
—From *The Story of a Soul: The Autobiography of St. Thérèse of Lisieux*

Δ As we pour out our feelings to God in all honesty, we also need to listen. At first we may only hear our own hollowness and emptiness and dryness. Maybe we will feel swallowed up in our painful feelings and have to move away from prayer and forget the process for a while because it is just too much. But we need to keep coming back. Gradually we will learn to hear God's quiet, gentle, persistent, hopeful voice.
—From *Praying Our Goodbyes* by Joyce Rupp

Δ My dear friend, I am the Lord who gives strength in the day of affliction. Come to me in times of trouble. The main thing that gets in the way of heavenly comfort is that you are slow in turning to prayer. Before you finally settle down for a serious talk with me, you look for all sorts of other comforts and you try to recover your spirits by keeping busy. So, it comes to pass that none of it helps very much until you remember that I am the one who rescues those who trust in me.
—From *The Imitation of Christ* by Thomas à Kempis

Δ True prayer brings us to the edge of a great mystery where we become inarticulate, where our knowledge fails.
—From *To Know As We Are Known* by Parker J. Palmer

Journaling: Ideas for Written Reflection

What is deepest inside you this week that you want to bring to God? Is it pain, joy, despair, or hope? Write an honest prayer to God about how you feel right now.

Prayers: For the World, for Others, for Myself

PRACTICING PRAYER:
On the Run

Opening Prayer
In the busyness of the day, let me stay close to you, God. Amen.

Scripture Focus
Keep these words that I am commanding you today in your heart. Recite them to your children and talk about them when you are at home and when you are away, when you lie down and when you rise. (Deuteronomy 6:6-7)

Daily Scripture Readings
Sunday	Deuteronomy 6:4-9
Monday	Romans 12:9-13
Tuesday	Hebrews 13:15
Wednesday	Ephesians 6:18
Thursday	1 Thessalonians 5:17-18
Friday	Philippians 4:4-7
Saturday	Luke 6:12-16

The Focus for Reflection

Almost every letter Paul wrote in the New Testament begins and ends with a word of grace. All except two of his letters begin with a prayer of thanksgiving and a promise of constant prayer for those to whom he is writing.

Hebrews 13:15 tells us to "continually" offer God "a sacrifice of praise," and 1 Thessalonians

5:17 says we should "pray without ceasing." Romans 12:12 urges us to "persevere in prayer." Ephesians 6 counsels us to "pray in the Spirit at all times."

In the Bible, believers prayed in prison, on a ship in the middle of a storm, in solitary places, alone, and in the middle of the busyness of the day.

Your days, both this summer and once classes start up at college this fall, will be full, rushed, overflowing with too much to do. The "busyness of the day" may well be the only time you have available for prayer. As you rush from one class to another, from one club meeting to the next study session, devote your hurriedness to God. This, in itself, is a form of prayer.

Mark says that Jesus often prayed at night (Mark 1:35; 6:46, 48). This was his time, the time, as Howard Thurman puts it, "for the long breath . . . when voices that had been quieted by the long day's work could once more be heard."

Yet Jesus too understood what it meant to pray constantly, throughout the day. For him, as for all believers, God breathes through all that is—through all the important, insignificant, joyous, and frightening things that happen in the course of a day. To be aware of God's presence in your life every day, all day, is to be practicing prayer even when you are on the run.

Points of Departure

Δ Prayer is not a withdrawal from life; it is a deeper involvement into life in accordance with

the motions of that spirit of Christ which rises
from within.
—From *A Life to Live—A Way to Pray* by John B. Coburn

Δ We must be ready to allow ourselves to be
interrupted by God.
—From *Life Together* by Dietrich Bonhoeffer

Δ If possible, before or during breakfast take a
few moments to think over tasks and experiences
that lie ahead for the day. Claim God's promise
that the divine love and light will go before you.
Visualize Christ already at your place of work,
filling it with light, healing and transforming the
experiences to come.

   This can be prayed while walking, driving, or
riding on the bus as well as while sitting in
stillness.
—From *Prayer, Stress, and Our Inner Wounds* by Flora
Slosson Wuellner

Δ When you light a candle, you begin to pray—
even if you never say a word or mention God's
name. Dinners by candlelight are innate prayer,
and birthday cakes when they shimmer with
candle fire are truly worship. . . . They are all
signs proclaiming that **God is with us**. Since
prayer means being in the presence of God, we
truly pray whenever we sense the Mystery.
—From *In Pursuit of the Great White Rabbit* by Edward Hays

Δ And then in bed; prayer is a goodnight,
almost as if to a roommate, and the final trust of

sleep, a "letting the world turn without you tonight."
—From *The Province Beyond the River* by W. Paul Jones

Journaling: Ideas for Written Reflection

What does it mean for you to "pray constantly" throughout the day? Do you find it hard or easy to stay focused on your spiritual life in the midst of the rest of your life? How does a strong prayer life help you to stay focused?

Prayers: For the World, for Others, for Myself

PRACTICING PRAYER:
On the Level

Opening Prayer
Help me to speak the truth to you this week, mighty and loving Creator. Amen.

Scripture Focus
O Lord, you have searched me and known me. (Psalm 139:1)

Daily Scripture Readings
Sunday	Psalm 139:1-12
Monday	1 John 5:13-15
Tuesday	Romans 8:26-27
Wednesday	John 17:20-23
Thursday	Luke 18:9-14
Friday	Psalm 86:1-7
Saturday	Matthew 7:7-8

The Focus for Reflection

Reporters say it to politicians when they want to get past the "official story" to something closer to the truth: "What can you tell me, strictly off the record?"

Strictly off the record. In confidence. Just between you and me. Not to be repeated. Things said quietly in private which are a step closer to the truth than things said out loud in public.

That's what it's like to practice prayer on the level. To cut through the first layers of the truth in order to get to the bare bones. To "level" with God and with yourself. To speak the truth about your thoughts, your feelings, your deeds, your desires.

Whether it is good news or bad news, glorious or unspeakable, God is there to receive you—all of you—in prayer. And when you give yourself fully, honestly, opening to God in prayer, the promise is sure and true and trustworthy. You are accepted by God, healed, loved.

Don't be afraid to practice prayer on the level. God will meet you wherever, however, whoever you are in the moment.

Points of Departure

Δ So cry whatever it is you want to cry—cry for help, cry for forgiveness, cry to give thanks, cry to ease pain, cry for joy, cry from anguish, cry from anger, cry from passion, cry for ecstasy, cry out of boredom, cry for love.
—From *A Life to Live—A Way to Pray* by John B. Coburn

Δ I think you cannot treat God with too much confidence. Tell [God] all that is in your heart.
—François Fénelon

Δ Christ loves the whole woman, the whole man.

Christ wants the whole woman, the whole man.

Christ loves and wants the whole of me, not the counterfeit self, not the pretend self, not the half self.
—From *Living with Contradiction* by Esther de Waal

Δ When I do something wrong I tend to alibi, to make excuses, blame someone else. Until I can accept whatever it is that I have done, I am only widening the gap between my real and my ontological self, and I am thus excluding myself so that I begin to think that I am unforgivable.
—From *A Circle of Quiet* by Madeleine L'Engle

Journaling: Ideas for Written Reflection

François Fénelon says that you cannot treat God with too much confidence. Is this true for you in your prayer life? What is easiest for you to share with God? What do you find more difficult to be honest with God about?

Prayer: For the World, for Others, for Myself

CHOICE MAKING

Opening Prayer

Gracious God, help me to see all my choices and to choose wisely this week. Amen.

Scripture Focus

For where your treasure is, there your heart will be also. (Matthew 6:21)

Daily Scripture Readings

Sunday	Joshua 24:14-18
Monday	Matthew 7:24-26
Tuesday	Deuteronomy 30:15-20
Wednesday	Genesis 3:1-7
Thursday	Psalm 27:4
Friday	John 10:10
Saturday	Proverbs 22:1-6

The Focus for Reflection

Can we establish one thing before we go any further? No matter how limiting a situation may seem, you/I/we all have choices. Those choices may not be ones we want, but we do always have choices.

The question, then, is not "Do I have a choice?" but "What choices do I have, and how do I best understand and choose among them?"

Jesus knew people had to make choices. He said, "I am the Way, the Truth, and the Life. No one comes to God except by me." For Jesus, the way to God was to be a follower of his. Direction, truth, and life were to be found through the direction, truth, and life of Jesus.

Given that, our choices suddenly have a framework for consideration. What else do we need to do, except to seek to know, understand, and apply the teachings of Jesus to our lives and our choice making?

What did Jesus teach? Begin your lifelong search to understand what he taught. How did Jesus live his life? Begin in your life to follow his life of prayer, reflection, and action.

Through seeking to know, understand, and follow the life of Jesus, God helps us to build a foundation from which choice making becomes less a burden and more an opportunity to grow closer to the God who seeks us.

Seek first the kingdom of God and God's rightness, and all other things—including good choices—will be added unto you.

Points of Departure

Δ I'm convinced that God communicates with us through the reasonableness of our own judgment, and we can trust it. The other alternative is to lay our judgment aside and take at full value what anyone tells you, and I'm not ready to do that.
—From *Why Do Mullet Jump?* by Gene Zimmerman

Δ Decision making, for the Iroquois, is an affair that reaches far beyond the moment and the limited concerns of those huddled around the campfire. When the Iroquois make their decisions, they do so always with the thought of honoring their ancestors and nurturing their unborn progeny. They ask: How does the decision we make today conform to the teachings of our grandparents and to the yearnings of our grandchildren?
—From *Time Wars* by Jeremy Rifkin

Δ Sometimes it must feel [confusing] to the beginning Christian. "Do this." "Do that." "Read your Bible." "Believe this." "Don't believe that." "Pray." I know from past experience how confusing all this can be.

Of course, we can't do it entirely on our own. We all need guidance and direction from those who have gone before us. This is one of the purposes of the church. In the end, however, we have to proceed on our own way, following the inner leading that God gives to those who seek God.
—From *Why Do Mullet Jump?* by Gene Zimmerman

Δ I am a writer who came of a sheltered life. A sheltered life can be a daring life as well. For all serious daring starts from within.
—From *One Writer's Beginnings* by Eudora Welty

Journaling: Ideas for Written Reflection

What is the most difficult choice you've ever had to make? How did you handle that choice? What choices are facing you this week and in the weeks ahead that you could use some help with?

Prayers: For the World, for Others, for Myself

WHO IS GOD?
Doing Your Own Theology

Opening Prayer

    God of many names, draw close to me. Amen.

Scripture Focus

    God said to Moses, "I AM WHO I AM."
(Exodus 3:14)

Daily Scripture Readings

Sunday	Deuteronomy 32:18
Monday	Matthew 6:9
Tuesday	1 John 4:8
Wednesday	Luke 13:34
Thursday	Exodus 3:13-15
Friday	Psalm 68:5
Saturday	Hebrews 12:29

The Focus for Reflection

Who first told you who God is? Your parents?
Teachers at school? Images from television?

If you were to draw a picture of your earliest
image of God, what would it be? An old man
with a white beard sitting on a throne? A pair of
all-seeing eyes, watching everything you do? The
hand of God reaching down to touch Adam's
hand on the ceiling of the Sistine Chapel? What if
you drew a picture of what God looks like to you
now? What would that picture be? An old man?
A pair of eyes?

Sometimes our experience of life changes and grows, but our notions of who God is may stagnate and atrophy.

In *Your God Is Too Small*, J.B. Phillips goes through a list of "unreal gods"—inadequate concepts of God which linger in our minds and which "prevent our catching a glimpse of the true God." Included in his list are God as the resident policeman, the parental hangover, the grand old man, the meek-and-mild, absolute perfection, heavenly bosom, God-in-a-box, managing director, and the second-hand God.

While some of the images contain a kernel of truth about God, many do not; they are all, in some sense, distortions. Phillips urges us to "fling wide the doors and windows of our minds and make some attempt to appreciate the 'size' of God."

To do this, Phillips says, we must be careful not to limit God to "religious matters." We must come to see and appreciate the incredibly broad sweep of this Creator's activity, the astonishing complexity of God's world, and the true simplicity of God's love.

A good place to start is with the Bible. The scriptures are filled with rich and varied images of God. God is a rock and a mother (Deut. 32:18), a shield and a sun (Ps. 84:11), refuge and shelter (Ps. 61:3-4), protector and father (Ps. 68:5), an expectant woman (Isa. 42:14), a shepherd (Ps. 23).

Another good place to start is with your own experience. When do you feel God's presence most powerfully? In the peaceful quiet at the end of the day . . . at the caring touch of a friend's

hand . . . in the sleepy pre-dawn warmth of just
waking up . . . in the power of Sunday
communion at church?

The creeds of the church reflect how the faith
community has seen God through the years. In
the second-century Apostle's Creed, God is
Father Almighty. In the Korean Creed (1930), God
is present in the "final triumph of righteousness."
In A Woman's Creed, written in 1983, God is in
the form of Jesus "who spoke of himself as a
mother hen who would gather her chicks under
her wing." In A New Creed of The United Church
of Canada, God is with us "in life, in death, in life
beyond death."

Use your mind, use your heart, use your
imagination. God is waiting to meet you in many
ways, many faces, sizes, shapes, and colors.
Praise be to God for the richness of God's self-
revelation!

Points of Departure

Δ God is no stranger to *feelings*. [God] knows
our whole range of emotions, because "in [God]
we live and move and have our being" (Acts
17:28).

In the Old Testament, God is pictured as
feeling anger (Exod. 4:14; Isa. 34:2), wrath (II
Kings 22:13; Ps. 90:7), hatred (Isa. 1:14; Amos
5:21), sorrow and grief (Gen. 6:6,7), displeasure
(Ps. 2:5; 60:1), jealousy (Exod. 20:5; Zeph. 1:18),
pity (Joel 2:18), compassion (Ps. 78:38; Mic. 7:19),
steadfast love (Exod. 34:6,7; Lam. 3:22), love (Hos.
11:1-4; Jer. 31:3), delight (Deut. 1:15), pleasure

(1 Chron. 29:17), patience (Jer. 15:15), and rejoicing (Isa. 65:19).
—From *Working Out Your Own Beliefs* by Douglas E. Wingeier

Δ All theology, like all fiction, is at its heart autobiography, and that what a theologian is doing essentially is examining as honestly as he [or she] can the rough-and-tumble of his [or her] own experience with all its ups and downs, its mysteries and loose ends, and expressing in logical, abstract terms the truths about human life and about God that he [or she] believes he [or she] has found implicit there.
—From *The Sacred Journey* by Frederick Buechner

Δ Theological inquiry is by no means a casual undertaking. It requires sustained disciplines of study, reflection, and prayer.

Yet the discernment of "plain truth for plain people" is not limited to theological specialists. Scholars have their role to play in assisting the people of God to fulfill this calling, but all Christians are called to theological reflection.
—From *The Book of Discipline of The United Methodist Church*, 1988

Journaling: Ideas for Written Reflection

What images of God do you most often use when you pray? What images mentioned in The Focus for Reflection are most unfamiliar to you?

Remember a time when you felt closest to God. What image of God comes to mind?

Remember a time when you felt lost, abandoned, far from God. What image comes to mind?

This week, choose an unfamiliar image of God and think about this facet of who God is as you pray. How does viewing God in this way affect your prayer life and your relationship with God?

Prayers: For the World, for Others, for Myself

STUDYING THE BIBLE:
Finding Yourself in the Faith Story

Opening Prayer

O God who speaks, let me listen to your Word. Amen.

Scripture Focus

Your word is a lamp to my feet and a light to my path. (Psalm 119:105)

Daily Scripture Readings

Sunday	John 1:1-5
Monday	Psalm 19:1-10
Tuesday	2 Timothy 3:16-17
Wednesday	Ezekiel 37:1-10
Thursday	Deuteronomy 6:4-9
Friday	2 Corinthians 3:2-3
Saturday	Deuteronomy 8:1-3

The Focus for Reflection

In my Sunday School class last week we were talking about the Bible—what it is, how often we read it, what we learn about ourselves through it. Our leader, a very serious and earnest man, began to recount solemnly how he often, in times of indecision, prayed that God would lead him to a passage of scripture that would be of help to him.

"Does it work?" asked a class member.

"Well, I thought so. But one day a few months back, I prayed for guidance from the Bible and the words *Isaiah 67:3* came into my head. I quickly got my Bible to look up the verse. When I turned to Isaiah, I discovered there were only 66 chapters," he laughed. "Maybe God was telling me to write chapter 67 myself!"

That's a good story. It reminds us of several things.

One, the Bible is an important book for telling us about God and guiding us in our faith journey—but we have to be careful about the questions we bring to it. We have to seek with an open mind—not a superstitious one. It's OK to bring doubts to Bible study. That's part of being open.

Two, the story of the people in the Bible is our story. Because the Bible is a collection of many people's stories—told over thousands of years—about their relationships with God, it might seem confusing at times. Different people experience God in different ways. But all the stories in the Bible share one thing in common: They are the story of the covenant between God and God's people. They are the story of the coming of God's son Jesus Christ. They are the story of how people break the covenant, over and over again, and of how God brings healing to the brokenness, over and over again.

Three, our life with God is reflected in the Bible's story of brokenness and healing. The story of our lives can be found in the stories of the Bible. We only have to look—prayerfully, carefully, daily.

God continues to speak of love, forgiveness, and grace through the Bible, through our lives, through people and events in the world today. The Bible is a record—a living record—of God's conversations with the people of God. The Bible is a record of our belief in Christ, God's best example of what it means to live life faithfully. The Bible is a gift from our spiritual ancestors inviting us to make their stories our stories, to learn from their experiences.

Those who do so discover the promise that a life viewed biblically is full of meaning, power, promise, and purpose.

Points of Departure

Δ The Bible is the frontier of the spirit where we must move and live in order to discover and to explore.
—From *God in Search of Man* by Abraham Joshua Heschel

Δ I searched it, I loved it, I believed it, but I did not think God stopped speaking to the human race when "the beloved disciple" finished his last book in the New Testament.
—From *Finding the Trail of Light* by Rufus M. Jones

Δ Take, for example, the narrow view many people have of the Bible. We like simple meanings and easy answers. . . .
. . . Many of its treasures are lost to those who bring to it only small questions. . . . If we treat the Bible like a railway timetable and ask of it

questions suited to such a document, we will get the response or revelation suited to our question.
—From *Soul Making* by Alan W. Jones

Δ O give me that book! At any price give me the Book of God! I have it. Here is knowledge enough for me. Let me be *homo unius libri* [a man of one book].
—John Wesley

Δ There is, in a word, nothing comfortable about the Bible—until we manage to get so used to it that we make it comfortable for ourselves. But then we are perhaps too used to it and too at home in it. Let us not be too sure we know the Bible just because we have learned not to be astonished at it, just because we have learned not to have problems with it. Have we perhaps learned at the same time not to really pay attention to it? Have we ceased to question the book and be questioned by it? Have we ceased to fight it? Then perhaps our reading is no longer serious.
—From *Opening the Bible* by Thomas Merton

Journaling: Ideas for Written Reflection

Can you remember a time when the Bible spoke to you? Which books or verses from the Bible are the most meaningful to you? What words of Jesus from the Bible are most significant for you? The most confusing? The most challenging?

Prayers: For the World, for Others, for Myself

LEAVING HOME:
What to Take Along, What to Leave Behind

Opening Prayer

Gracious and loving God, you have been a good and generous presence in my life. Be here, now, that I may know again the goodness of your care for me, in all things. Amen.

Scripture Focus

Lord, you have been a home for us,
> For one generation after another.
>> (Psalm 90:1)
>>> (from *The Psalms: A New Translation for Prayer and Worship* by Gary Chamberlain)

Daily Scripture Readings

Sunday	Genesis 12:1-9
Monday	Exodus 13:18-22
Tuesday	Joshua 24:14-18
Wednesday	Psalm 139:1-12
Thursday	Matthew 7:24-27/Luke 6:46-49
Friday	Luke 8:4-15
Saturday	Philippians 1:3-11

The Focus for Reflection

Leave-taking. Hurried good-byes to family, friends, and all that is familiar. Whether you're leaving home to go to college for the semester as a resident student or for the day as a commuter, "home" will never be the same again.

Leave-takings are seldom easy, for they mean exchanging the known for the unknown, the familiar for the unfamiliar, the old and comfortable for the new and strange. Yet the Book of Psalms, in the passage above, offers an assurance that wherever you go, you take "home" with you. Read the passage from Psalm 90 at the beginning of this section again.

This psalm is a promise, a reminder, that the constancy that is God goes with you to college. Amid all the changes, all the strangeness, all the newness, God is there as an anchor, a familiar friend, an old and trusted companion. It's a bit like setting out on a long journey into uncharted territory, but knowing that you're wearing the sturdy, comfortable hiking shoes that have seen you over many rugged miles and that you're carrying the reliable compass that has guided you surely, steadily, in the past.

What to take along, what to leave behind as you set out from home to college? You've probably gotten a lot of advice about the practical things—clothes, books, computer, towels and sheets, running shoes, hair dryer, tape player, clock radio. What about the other things—the intangibles, things that you can't pack in a suitcase or a box, but stuff that you want to be sure to take along with you?

Like the encouragement and love of family and friends. The best wishes and prayers of your faith community at home. The courage you need to leave home, take risks, and grow. The spiritual disciplines and prayer life that sustain and nurture you. Joy and excitement at the new challenges before you. A sense of humor—one that will get you through a multitude of "learning experiences."

And what to leave behind? Some of the baggage, the junk you know you've been accumulating, stuff that weighs you down. On the practical side, this might mean tossing out your collection of Bart Simpson paraphernalia, leaving behind the costume you wore in the senior play, or giving away your rock and mineral display from junior high science class.

On the other side, it might mean getting rid of some less tangible things. Like your tendency to procrastinate, to put off doing things you don't particularly like to do. It may mean getting rid of some outdated notions about yourself—that you can't do anything right, or that you always have to do everything perfectly. It may be time to leave behind some old feelings of guilt, to forgive yourself for things you've done that you wish you hadn't, to move on with a lighter load.

Leaving home. An important bend in the road. Time to take stock, to take leave, to take off on your own. What to take along, what to leave behind? When the time comes to pack up and go, seek the guidance of God, and of people you trust. The answers will come, in God's own time. That is the promise of the faith.

And on the journey toward whatever is next in your life, the constancy that is God travels with you. As you seek to create or to re-create your home in a new place, remember the "home" that God is for you, and has been for generation after

generation of the faithful who left the familiarity
of one home to start another.

Points of Departure

Δ Where we love is home,
Home that our feet may leave, but not our
      hearts.
—From "Homesick in Heaven" by Oliver Wendell Holmes

Δ When the time came to leave for Jacksonville,
I packed a borrowed old trunk with no lock and
no handles, roped it securely, said my good-byes,
and left for the railway station. When I bought
my ticket, the agent refused to check my trunk on
my ticket because the regulations stipulated that
the check must be attached to the trunk handle,
not to a rope. The trunk would have to be sent
express but I had no money except for a dollar
and a few cents left after I bought my ticket.

I sat down on the steps of the railway station
and cried my heart out. Presently I opened my
eyes and saw before me a large pair of work
shoes. My eyes crawled upward until I saw the
man's face. He was a black man, dressed in
overalls and a denim cap. As he looked down at
me he rolled a cigarette and lit it. Then he said,
"Boy, what in hell are you crying about?"

And I told him.

"If you're trying to get out of this damn town
to get an education, the least I can do is to help
you. Come with me," he said.

He took me around to the agent and asked, "How much does it take to send this boy's trunk to Jacksonville?"

Then he took out his rawhide money bag and counted the money out. When the agent handed him the receipt, he handed it to me. Then, without a word, he turned and disappeared down the railroad track. I never saw him again.

—From *With Head and Heart* by Howard Thurman

Journaling: Ideas for Written Reflection

Take some time to consider what you want to take with you from home and what you want to leave behind as you head off to school. Make a list of these "intangibles" for yourself. Are some things on your list harder to take with you or to leave behind than you thought they'd be?

Reflect on the ways God has been with you on your life's journey this far. Are there people, places, incidents in your life that witness to God's presence with you? How does God's presence in your past affect your feelings about moving on toward an unknown future?

Prayers: For the World, for Others, for Myself

CHANGE:
Finding Your Way in a New Place

Opening Prayer

Changeless God, stay by my side through all the changes of my life. Amen.

Scripture Focus

We will all be changed . . . (1 Corinthians 15:51)

Daily Scripture Readings

Sunday	Luke 2:41-52
Monday	Psalm 102:25-28
Tuesday	1 Corinthians 15:51-58
Wednesday	Genesis 17:1-5, 15-16
Thursday	Matthew 2:18-25
Friday	Jeremiah 31:31-34
Saturday	1 Corinthians 13:11-12

The Focus for Reflection

"There will be moments when everything goes well; don't worry, it won't last." That was the tongue-in-cheek advice of my favorite high school teacher as I went off to college. Unlike some of the other advice I was given at the time, it later turned out to be true.

College—especially that first year—always seemed to me to be something between crisis and opportunity. People eagerly told me that I would find myself on the growing edge of life, but they

77

didn't tell me I would sometimes also find myself simply on the edge. They told me to be myself, but they didn't tell me there would be times when I didn't like the self I was being, and when I would want to be, instead, someone else.

Change. It is inevitable. In point of fact, the only thing constant in life is change. The ancient philosopher Heraclitus said it wasn't possible for one person to step into the same river twice—both the person and the river change from moment to moment.

Change—in yourself, in your circumstances, and in your way of looking at things—is inevitable. Facing personal changes in the midst of a changing world can be painful. It is sometimes frightening to go from what is comfortable and familiar to what is new and unfamiliar. Moving through change is the process of living in the transition place between giving up the old and finding your place in the new.

Learning itself is a process of change. Richard Strozzi Heckler says in *The Anatomy of Change* that in order to learn, you must to a certain degree let go of who you think you are and what you think you know. This transition, from what you are to what you can become, is where you learn.

You are not alone on this journey of change. Jim Henson, creator of the Muppets, believed that life, for him, was a process of growth. "I can't help but think of myself as a very 'human' being," he said. "I have the full complement of weaknesses, fears, problems, ego, sensuality, etc. But again, I think this is why we're here—to work our way through all this and to hopefully come out a bit wiser and better for having gone through it all."

Jesus, too, is your companion on this journey. The scriptures say that he too experienced change. "And Jesus grew in wisdom and stature." As he moved through life, he met new circumstances, new relationships, new situations—challenges to change. It wasn't always easy for him; he wasn't always sure of himself. Perhaps the most difficult change he faced was his decision in the garden of Gethsemane—the challenge to discern and follow God's will for him, all the way through the cross to resurrection.

The Bible itself is the story of a people called to change. Abram and Sarai traveled to a new country, with changed names to mark their journey. In the Hebrew scriptures, an encounter with God meant profound personal and social change. In the New Testament, people's interactions with Jesus and his disciples resulted in changed lives.

Crisis. Opportunity. Change. It's inevitable on this journey called life. In the middle of the confusion and the chaos and the opportunities of change, remember that you are not alone. God—and some faithful fellow-journeyers—are with you through all the changes.

Points of Departure

Δ Once you are in college, you will quite suddenly be in the midst of a new and probably unfamiliar environment. This takes some adjusting for everyone.

In college a large number of people with very different personalities, backgrounds, and personal histories are thrown together. New Yorkers suddenly meet people from Amarillo, Boise, and Bangor. Farm people encounter city dwellers. Rich and poor share the same classes and dorms. This diversity, plus the suddenness with which you are all thrown together, and the sheer number of people going to college together, can be disorienting, confusing, and even frightening at first.

This is more or less to be expected. Don't get overwhelmed by the new environment, all that diversity, and all those people. Dip into it at whatever speed suits you best. Go slow if you need to. You'll be able to adjust as time passes.
—From *College: A User's Manual* by Scott Edelstein

Δ Accustomed as we are to change, or unaccustomed, we think of a change of heart, of clothes, of life, with some uncertainty. We put off the old, put on the new, yet say that the more it changes the more it remains the same. Every age is an age of transition.
—From *Poetry and Change* by Josephine Miles

Δ God, grant me the serenity to accept the things I cannot change, the courage to change the things I can, and the wisdom to know the difference.
—Reinhold Niebuhr

Journaling: Ideas for Written Reflection

Some changes are easier to cope with than others. Some seem easy, natural—like changing your hair or the way you dress. Others are bigger, more frightening—like watching your relationship with your parents change or feeling some of your basic beliefs challenged. Take a few moments to sit quietly and reflect. What changes are you facing right now that seem easy and natural? Which seem bigger and a bit more frightening?

Prayers: For the World, for Others, for Myself

LOVING GOD WITH YOUR MIND:
The Sacredness of Study

Opening Prayer

Wise and holy God, I praise you with all my being—heart, soul, body, and mind. Amen.

Scripture Focus

You shall love the Lord your God with all your heart, and with all your soul, and with all your mind. (Matthew 22:37)

Daily Scripture Readings

Sunday	Matthew 22:34-40
Monday	Psalm 119:33-40
Tuesday	Philippians 4:8-9
Wednesday	Matthew 11:29
Thursday	Romans 11:33-36
Friday	Ephesians 4:17-24
Saturday	Philippians 1:9-11

The Focus for Reflection

"The life of the mind." A college professor I once had used to talk about "the life of the mind" every year at the beginning of classes.

At the time, it evoked images of a science fiction movie for me, "Who knows what lurks in the life of the mind?" Pretty scary stuff, to my already overstimulated first-week-in-college imagination.

Later on that year, and over the course of the next three, I began to get a glimmer of what my professor was talking about. Sitting in the library late one night, struggling over a complex programming exercise, the wonders of the computer's language suddenly came clear. Staring at a math problem until the solution crystallized itself on the page. The insight into the workings of one particular e.e. cummings' poem. The questions of the history professor that compelled us to search for new answers, new notions, new ideas.

So that's what he meant: the life of the mind. Learning gives way to insight and insight gives birth to joy and wonder. Discipline. Imagination.

Your life's work at present, your vocation right now, is to be a student. To study, to learn, to question, to challenge, to imagine, to stretch the limits of knowledge. The exercise of the mind, the vision of the mind's eye—these are surely holy ways to love God. Your studies will raise questions and doubts. Jesus always welcomed questions and doubts in his followers.

Revel in your studies, even when they threaten to overwhelm you. Consecrate your desk, even when you don't want to spend time there. Make your textbooks holy vessels. Confess ignorance, receive God's invitation to learn, use the power of your imagination. Love God with your mind.

Points of Departure

Δ Life in college is not all struggle and challenge and courage. The transitions you face will also yield grand new discoveries about yourself, about your faith, about the world. Take time to celebrate, to laugh, to rejoice in the gift of being a student.
—From *Singing in a Strange New Land* by Helen R. Neinast

Δ It is true that minds are of different sizes, just as bodies are of different sizes. But it is also true that minds are of different *shapes*, just as bodies are of different shapes. And the shape can be as important as the size. . . .

The people I most enjoy are not necessarily those with the largest mentalities, but those who know how to use what they have with charm, humor, and individuality. A four-cylinder mind, properly tuned and expertly driven, can generally run rings around an eight-cylinder mind that is cumbersome and self-satisfied.
—From *The Best of Sydney J. Harris*

Δ Education—the good education, that is—can help us to move out beyond the narrow and calcifying confines of the ego so that we can identify ourselves sympathetically—no, that word is not strong enough—identify ourselves *compassionately* with the mainstream of humanity.
—From *Human Options* by Norman Cousins

Δ The most worthwhile form of education is the kind that puts the educator inside you, as it were, so that the appetite for learning persists long after the external pressure for grades and degrees has vanished. Otherwise you are not educated; you are merely trained.
—From *Pieces of Eight* by Sydney J. Harris

Δ Academic work is one of those fields containing a pearl so precious that it is worth while to sell all our possessions, keeping nothing for ourselves, in order to be able to acquire it.
—From *Waiting for God* by Simone Weil

Journaling: Ideas for Written Reflection
Sometimes being in school feels like a blessing. Sometimes it feels like a curse. Write a prayer of thanksgiving for those times when you have felt blessed to be a student, and keep it handy for those times when it's harder to be grateful for your current vocation.

Prayers: For the World, for Others, for Myself

THE HOLINESS OF TIME:
Time Management from a Faith Perspective

Opening Prayer

O timeless, eternal God, Creator of all the hours of the day and of the night, I offer up to you those things which claim my time, and ask your guidance as I live each day of my life. Amen.

Scripture Focus

For everything there is a season, and a time for every matter under heaven. (Ecclesiastes 3:1)

Daily Scripture Readings

Sunday	Genesis 1:31–2:3
Monday	Luke 13:10-17
Tuesday	Isaiah 58:13-14
Wednesday	Mark 2:23-28
Thursday	Ecclesiastes 3:1-8
Friday	Luke 12:22-31
Saturday	2 Peter 3:8-13

The Focus for Reflection

Ben Franklin knew it: "Time is money." Chaucer wrote about it: "Time lost may not recovered be." Eugene Ionesco put it most succinctly: "We haven't the time to take our time."

As a first-year college student, you have no doubt discovered the dilemma of time. You have to balance the time demands that family, friends, extracurricular activities, studies, and roommates place on your day. College students engage in "time wars," battling the clock to organize, reorganize, spend, and save time. Especially this first year, you will struggle with the time pressures of new opportunities to learn, play, work, study, serve.

There are dozens of books, philosophies, advice-givers, workshops, and organizers to help you manage your time. Day-Runners, Day-Timers, Fil-o-Fax . . . the list of tools goes on and on.

Odette Lockwood-Stewart, campus minister at the University of California at Los Angeles, asks the question that is at the heart of our relationship with time: "What do we do with the time we save through hurry, technology, schedules, and clever calendars? . . . What might our calendars and datebooks reveal about the meaning of the book our days are writing?"

Categories like "sacred" and "secular" simply do not apply to the minutes, hours, and days of our lives. Morning and night, work time and play—it is all sacred.

In the middle of your hectic schedule, remember that. All time is holy . . . and, because of that, to manage and to care for your time is a holy act. Don't let the urgent things crowd out the important ones. Take time, each day, to discern the difference between the two.

Points of Departure

Δ I have taken time off. Literally. The watch that straps my workaday wrist to its demands sits on the kitchen shelf.

I have shed its manufactured time, its minute hand, hour hand, just the way I shed my city wardrobe. . . . Gradually, I have even begun to lose track of time. First the minute and then the hour, finally the day. My watch and I have wound down.

I reckon my real vacation from the moment I forget whether it is Thursday or Friday. And the moment I realize that it doesn't make any difference. At last, I tell myself, I have slipped out of one time frame and sunk into another one. I have left a world divided by nothing more than numbers, sixty minutes, twenty-four hours, seven days a week. I have entered a world of seasons: blueberry, raspberry, blackberry season; lobsters that shed old shells and then harden new ones. My daily life here is more connected to the tide than the time.

—From *Making Sense* by Ellen Goodman

Δ *Homo sapiens* is, in the words of the scientist Alfred Korzybski, the only "time-binding" animal. All of our perceptions of self and world are mediated by the way we imagine, explain, use, and implement time. Time is at once both dazzling and versatile, enigmatic and vexing. We can look ahead of ourselves, we can steal our way

back into the past, we can detach ourselves from the moment and look at ourselves from a distance.
—From *Time Wars* by Jeremy Rifkin

Δ *Carpe diem*. Seize the day.
—Horace

Δ A sweet summer afternoon. Cool breezes and a clear sky. This day will not come again.

The young bulls lie under a tree in the corner of their field.

Quiet afternoon. Blue hills. Day lilies nod in the wind.

This day will not come again.
—From *Conjectures of a Guilty Bystander* by Thomas Merton

Δ Ultimately, Indian time is a concept based on a sense of propriety, on a ritual understanding of order and harmony. For an Indian, if being on time means being out of harmony with self and ritual, the Indian will be "late." The right timing for a tribal Indian is the time when he or she is in balance with the flow of the four rivers of life. That is, Indian time rests on a perception of individuals as part of an entire gestalt in which fittingness is not a matter of how gear teeth mesh with each other but rather how the person meshes with the revolving of the seasons, the land, and the mythic reality that shapes all life into significance.
—From *The Sacred Hoop* by Paula Gunn Allen

Journaling: Ideas for Written Reflection

Try an experiment. Keep a record of your activities for one day, or for a whole week. At the end of that time, look back to see if you can identify which values are expressed in your use of time. Ask yourself these questions:

>What took too much of my time? What took too little?

>How much time did I spend nurturing my body? My spirit?

>When did I feel unfocused about the way I spent my time?

>When did I feel focused and "in charge"?

Prayers: For the World, for Others, for Myself

SHRINKING EXPECTATIONS

Opening Prayer

God, help me to rely on your strength and grace to sustain me every day. Amen.

Scripture Focus

The Lord is my shepherd. (Psalm 23:1)

Daily Scripture Readings

Sunday	Matthew 11:25-30
Monday	Romans 5:18-21
Tuesday	Psalm 23
Wednesday	Matthew 1:18-25
Thursday	1 Peter 5:7
Friday	1 Samuel 17:41-49
Saturday	Revelation 3:20

The Focus for Reflection

The movie was violent, at times difficult to watch; yet a line from it will stay with me for a long time. Clint Eastwood had defeated yet another "bad guy" when he said, "A man's got to know his limitations."

The movie's content and drive may be debatable, but this line has a ring of truth. Personalize this statement, and it becomes an important lifeline: "I've got to know my limita-tions."

No matter how hard you study, work, exercise, recreate, pray, love, worship . . . you have limitations.

Now put a new "frame" around it. We all have capabilities and interests that take us in different directions. This is part of God's creation.

The Gospel of Luke tells us that Jesus "increased in wisdom and in years, and in divine and human favor." It seems obvious that as Jesus grew, so did his understanding of his capabilities and interests and his knowledge of God's direction for his life. Often we find Jesus in prayer, meditation, conversation. At times Jesus was tempted, struggled, needed time alone. The angels ministered to him. Yes, even he felt the limits of life on this earth.

Where do your gifts lie? What are your interests? What are you capable of doing? Answers to these questions will give you insight into your personal expectations and limitations. Knowing both capabilities and limitations will help you set up expectations for yourself and others.

Suppose a friend told you that they expected to get a 1500 on the SAT and if they did not they would be disappointed in themselves. Right— you would think this a foolish expectation.

How about all A's in college, running a hundred yards in five seconds flat, memorizing the dictionary? These are not reasonable expectations.

What about being liked by everybody, never getting angry, having the perfect body, never sinning? Expectations guaranteed to disappoint!

Most of us are faced with an ongoing challenge to have reasonable expectations of ourselves. God calls us to a discipline of prayer, study, and love to help us gain an understanding of what we might reasonably expect of ourselves.

You and I are not going to run a hundred yards in five seconds—at least I am not. But, you and I can travel a faith journey together with God, coming to know what gifts God's grace has given us, in what directions God leads us, and what we may reasonably expect from ourselves in response to God's love.

You will be good at some things, okay at others, not so hot at still others. (How is your pole vault these days?) The challenge is simple and clear. Discover your gifts and interests, develop those gifts and interests, use them all.

College is a great time to learn about yourself and your place in God's creation. It makes sense to challenge yourself, but don't defeat yourself by setting up expectations you cannot meet.

Career, commitment, relationships, marriage, family, education, spirituality, growth. The faith journey will challenge you to set up expectations along the way. Make sure they are fair, reasonable, and reflect God's gifts to you. If not, shrink them down to a reasonable size. Then, let go and let God guide you.

Points of Departure

Δ I'm not sure God put us here to do everything "just right." If so, most of us are poorly equipped for perfection. We come closer to understanding ourselves when we can see and accept some of our human limitations.

This isn't an invitation to pass off every failure by claiming imperfection or to avoid trying; but rather it is advice that we need to accept some imperfection and acknowledge that we can't do it all right all the time.

The encouraging thing about this reality is that God loves us and meets us at these places of imperfection with grace and strength.
—From *Why Do Mullet Jump?* by Gene Zimmerman

Δ When we set unattainable goals, we automatically position ourselves to fail and become discouraged. When we push beyond our limits, we cheat ourselves out of the chance to feel good about our accomplishments. . . .

If we want to get back to enjoying our activities, we have to stop putting so much pressure on ourselves.
—From *A New Day*

Journaling: Ideas for Written Reflection
In what areas do you expect too much of yourself? Too little? Reflect on the ways your expectations of yourself are either unfair or balanced.

Prayers: For the World, for Others, for Myself

LIFE IN THE BALANCE

Opening Prayer
Sure and steady God, keep me balanced.
Amen.

Scripture Focus
For everything there is a season. (Ecclesiastes 3:1)

Daily Scripture Readings
Sunday	Psalm 23
Monday	Colossians 3:1-4
Tuesday	Matthew 13:1-9
Wednesday	Ecclesiastes 3:1-8
Thursday	Psalm 100
Friday	1 Corinthians 12:14-16
Saturday	Luke 7:31-35

The Focus for Reflection

How do you measure mental and spiritual health? This question is one that may be shortened to "What is normal?" Or, better yet, "Am I normal?"

Tough questions. Often asked. Real hard to measure.

Sigmund Freud believed that mental health could be evaluated by knowing how an individual is doing in the areas of work, love, and play. Are these three in balance? Are these three

97

fulfilling? For Freud, the answers to these questions in the affirmative is a key sign of mental health.

A student of Freud, Alfred Adler, felt that while Freud had included three key fundamentals of mental health, he had left out one—social interest. Was a person reaching out beyond herself or himself to be a helpful part of the society at large? For Adler, work, love, and play had to be in balance with social responsibility for a person to be fully healthy and normal.

To this list of four, we would add spirituality as a fifth measure. What is the quality of your relationship with God? Because God is the God of creation and goes before us, is with us, and stands ready to meet us, you already have a relationship with God. How is it going?

Take some time to sit back and evaluate these five areas of your life—love, work, play, social responsibility, and spirituality. You can use an imaginary scale of one to ten, with one being almost nonexistent and ten being everything you ever wanted it to be.

How did it come out? If there are areas you're not satisfied with, then you have some changes to make to get your life more in balance. Take it easy. Take it one category at a time. Find a good balance. Enlist God's help and the help of good friends in the faith. Be honest with yourself. Evaluate fairly. Learn and grow.

Points of Departure

Δ To stay in touch with laughter and tears is to be informed by each and imprisoned by neither. To laugh all the time is mockery; to cry continually leads to self-pity and destruction. When joy and sorrow inform each other, and neither is forgotten, we find freedom and balance.
—From *Why Do Mullet Jump?* by Gene Zimmerman

Δ Or another way to think about this [balance] might be to reflect on the rhythmic alternation which governs the whole of life. Throughout the Rule [of St. Benedict] we are made aware of the conflicting demands of body, mind and spirit, and of the need to pay attention to their contrasting claims. There must be time to work, time to study and time to pray. . . . Life is inextricably bound up in the alternation of day and night, of the changing seasons, of the ebb and flow of the seasons, of the changing shape of the liturgical year. This way of life brings us into touch with the rhythm inherent in all things, in the holding together of the contradiction of growth and decline, of light and dark, of dying and rising again.
—From *Living with Contradiction* by Esther de Waal

Δ Like the birth of a baby or the opening of a rose, the birth of the true self takes place in God's time. We must wait for God, we must be awake; we must trust in [God's] hidden action within us.
—From *Merton's Palace of Nowhere* by James Finley

Δ The sweetness needs salt for taste, the light needs the darkness for contrast, the individual needs the society, the pursuit of competition requires the restraint of cooperation, the masculine personality in men must be tempered by some feminine traits, just as the feminine personality must be endowed with some masculine traits, or both become monsters and not human beings.

—From *The Authentic Person* by Sydney J. Harris

Journaling: Ideas for Written Reflection

How did you score on the self-evaluation in the Focus for Reflection? What can you do to get things in your life—work, school, relationships—more in balance?

Prayers: For the World, for Others, for Myself

LIFE IN THE BALANCE:
Love and Relationships

Opening Prayer

Befriend me this week as I befriend others, Holy Spirit. Amen.

Scripture Focus

When I remember you in my prayers, I always thank my God. (Philemon 4)

Daily Scripture Readings

Sunday	Ephesians 4:1-7
Monday	Proverbs 17:17
Tuesday	John 13:34-35
Wednesday	Romans 16:1-16
Thursday	1 Samuel 17:55–18:5
Friday	Ruth 1:15-18
Saturday	Philemon 1-7

The Focus for Reflection

There are many areas where Christianity and psychology stand on common ground. Perhaps the most important area of agreement is the place of love and relationship. All the mainline psychological theories agree that love and relationship are a key part of mental health. Without these loving relationships, a balanced life is at risk.

Whether you read Leviticus or Deuteronomy in the Hebrew Scriptures or Matthew, Luke,

101

Corinthians, or First John in the New Testament, it is obvious that the Bible teaches the importance of loving relationships.

God created each of us with a basic need to love and be loved. It is that simple. We all need the care and affection of others, and, likewise, we need to care for and about others.

You may not have noticed yet, but every relationship you have changes. Try as you might to keep your world neat and predictable, relationships change. In fact, the more emotionally invested you are with someone, the surer and more obvious the changes will be. The changes may not be easy, but they are necessary for the relationship to grow and survive.

So there it is: We all need loving relationships, and all relationships are guaranteed to change. Here's some help in dealing with those facts. Jesus showed what God asks of us in relationships. We all have been blessed with a capacity to love with our heart, our soul, our mind, and our strength. God asks us to make our best effort to love with all our being.

We have a tremendous capacity to bless God by accepting God's love for us and loving God back with our heart, soul, mind, and strength. This is the best foundation we can have in other relationships.

There will be times when you will be hurt or your trust will be broken. Yet, what comes through with certainty is that God yearns for your life to be filled with chances to be in loving relationships. What better way to express your love than to love God back and to give and receive love with others?

Points of Departure

Δ We have all known the long loneliness and we have learned that the only solution is love and that love comes with community.
—From *The Long Loneliness* by Dorothy Day

Δ Yes, the highest sign of friendship is that of giving another the privilege of sharing your inner thought.
—From *The Meaning of Gifts* by Paul Tournier

Δ Baptism is a sacrament of friendship. Through it we are anointed to relationship with our brothers and sisters in the Christian community. The anointing is a sign of the strength that we can receive from God and each other.
—From *Called to Be Friends* by Paula Ripple

Δ Jesus placed great value on relationships. He chose to spend much of his time deepening his connections with a few significant persons rather than addressing the crowds. What is more, his teaching was filled with practical suggestions on how to befriend people and how to relate to friends.
—From *The Friendship Factor* by Alan Loy McGinnis

Journaling: Ideas for Written Reflection

Are relationships an important part of your life? Are there people in your life who love and care for you, and for whom you do the same? How much time do you invest in relationships?

Prayers: For the World, for Others, for Myself

LIFE IN THE BALANCE:
The Refreshment of Play and Rest

Opening Prayer

Give me laughter. Give me play. Give me rest. Amen.

Scripture Focus

David danced before the Lord with all his might. (2 Samuel 6:14)

Daily Scripture Readings

Sunday	Ephesians 5:18-20
Monday	1 Thessalonians 5:16
Tuesday	Psalm 92:1-4
Wednesday	Jeremiah 31:26
Thursday	2 Samuel 6:12-15
Friday	Psalm 65:9-13
Saturday	Zechariah 8:3-5

The Focus for Reflection

During football games at the University of North Carolina in Chapel Hill, fans perform what they call the "silent cheer." At a count of three, about twenty-five or thirty thousand people stand up and do the most energetic and frenetic cheer humanly possible. Up to their feet they leap, mouths wide open, arms flailing, hopping up and down. But the "cheer" is absolutely silent—no noise comes from their open mouths, and their hands don't make any clapping sound.

I love it. People having fun . . . people playing.

Play, rest, recreation, re-creation—call it what you will. Every competent psych-type will tell you that one of the key elements of mental health is play and rest. If we don't get adequate amounts of both, our mental and spiritual health is at risk.

Many times in the Gospels we find Jesus seeking time away—in a boat, on a mountain, in a garden, by the seashore. Jesus in the fullness of his humanity rested, played, re-created.

There are lots of ways to rest and gain renewal. Some people hit and follow a little white golf ball around a 7,000-yard course. Others climb to the top of a hill and meditate. Some go across town or across the country to build a house for people who don't have one.

Sometimes, we work so hard at play and rest that we come back stressed and tired. I believe that intention and structure are key to play and rest. Ask yourself some questions: Is this activity intended to be recreational, or do I have a tremendous ego, financial, or interpersonal investment in it? For play and rest to be truly re-creative, it needs to be as unencumbered of all these "extras" as possible.

The day I saw my first "silent cheer," I learned something new about what fun play could be. Nonsensical, collective, and just plain silly.

Keep searching until you find a good level of play and rest. Do something just for the fun of it.

Points of Departure

Δ When King David's wife berates him for making a fool of himself by leaping and dancing before the ark of the Lord with all his might, he protests by saying that it seemed exactly the right thing to do considering all the Lord had done for him. "Therefore will I play before the Lord," he tells her (2 Samuel 6:14-21).
—From *Whistling in the Dark* by Frederick Buechner

Δ Most middle-class Americans tend to worship their work, to work at their play, and to play at their worship.
—From *Work, Play and Worship in a Leisure-Oriented Society* by Gordon Dahl

Δ Every day of your life take at least an hour's exercise . . . If you can, take it in the open air.
—John Wesley

Δ What is serious to us is often very trivial in the sight of God. What in God might appear to us as "play" is perhaps what God . . . takes most seriously.
—From *New Seeds of Contemplation* by Thomas Merton

Δ It is ever a grace and a benediction to be able to come to a halt, to stop, to pause, to make a rest of motion.
—From *The Inward Journey* by Howard Thurman

Journaling: Ideas for Written Reflection

Make a list of things you like to do for fun and to relax. Make a list of the "restful" people and places in your life. Keep track this week of how often you do these things or visit these people and places.

Prayers: For the World, for Others, for Myself

LIFE IN THE BALANCE:
Reaching Beyond Yourself

Opening Prayer

Let me respond to your love by loving others.
Amen.

Scripture Focus

Who is my neighbor? (Luke 10:29)

Daily Scripture Readings

Sunday	Job 2:11-13
Monday	2 Kings 3:1-10
Tuesday	Luke 16:25-32
Wednesday	Esther 4:11–5:3
Thursday	Isaiah 36:1-2
Friday	Matthew 25:31-46
Saturday	Luke 10:29-37

The Focus for Reflection

In the middle of class schedules, work, close
relationships, and play, be sure to include time
for "reaching beyond yourself." Finding the
energy and interest to reach out to others is an
important way to maintain good mental and
spiritual health.

Throughout the Bible we find constant
examples of the call that each of us has to reach
out to others. The helping, caring, and loving of
others is a great way to bless God. It is a fitting
response to God's love.

We know that John Wesley believed and taught that "good works" naturally spring from our faith in Jesus Christ. Many counselors will tell you that a helpful treatment for depression is simply to reach out and care for another.

Perhaps you could reach beyond yourself and just listen to someone who is hurting, physically or spiritually. Or you could become involved in a group that seeks to meet some of the emotional and physical needs of others. Check to see what your campus ministry is doing to help others.

Or look into joining a work team over spring break. There are lots of organizations that need your volunteer time as you seek to reach out.

Clearly Jesus taught us that whoever is in need is also our neighbor, the neighbor we are called to love.

Points of Departure

Δ In Jesus' parable of the last judgment (Matthew 25:31-46) a clear distinction was made among all who were there. The separation was between those who cared and those who didn't. That, according to the parable, is the sole determination of the judgment: whether you are for or against your brothers and sisters, whether you are here just to help yourself or to help anyone you can.

It appears that God doesn't judge us. We judge ourselves. God merely pronounces the judgment when the time comes.

—From *Why Do Mullet Jump?* by Gene Zimmerman

Δ You say: "But how can I serve the Lord? I'm not important. What I do is so common and of little consequence. Anyone can do what I do."

But I say to you: "Every time you meet another human being you have the opportunity. It's a chance at holiness. For you will do one of two things, then. Either you will build [that person] up, or you will tear [that person] down. . . . You will create, or you will destroy. And the things you dignify or deny are God's own property. They are made, each one of them, in [God's] own image."
—From *Ragman and Other Cries of Faith* by Walter Wangerin, Jr.

Δ I've always been taught there were two great commandments: Love the Lord thy God with all thy heart, mind, soul, and strength; and love thy neighbor as thyself. And so I think that sums the whole thing up pretty doggoned good. If we would do that, boy, would this world be a lot easier.
—From an interview with Bobby Bowden, head football coach at Florida State University

Δ Christ has no body now on earth but yours;
    yours are the only hands with which he can
        do his work,
    yours are the only feet with which he can go
        about the world,
    yours are the only eyes through which his
        compassion
    can shine forth upon a troubled world.

Christ has no body now on earth but yours.
—St. Teresa of Avila

Journaling: Ideas for Written Reflection

How is God calling you to reach out beyond yourself this week? How does it feel to reach beyond yourself to another?

Prayers: For the World, for Others, for Myself

SEXUALITY:
God's Amazing Gift

Opening Prayer

Thank you, God, for the gift of my body.
Amen.

Scripture Focus

Let love be genuine. (Romans 12:9)

Daily Scripture Readings

Sunday	Genesis 1:27, 31
Monday	1 John 3:18
Tuesday	Romans 12:1-3
Wednesday	Genesis 2:18-25
Thursday	1 Timothy 4:12
Friday	Song of Solomon 2:8-17
Saturday	1 Corinthians 6:12-20

The Focus for Reflection

Our sexuality is a good and great gift. With
this gift comes an opportunity to relate to another
in a very special way. The gift is different for each
of us, yet our sexuality has many common
threads.

This gift may hurt or heal, shatter or make
whole, affirm or destroy. It is a gift of pleasure
that may contribute to intimacy with another. It is
a gift that reaches beyond its most basic form and
impacts us—spiritually, psychologically,

physically, emotionally, intellectually, ethically, and socially.

Sexuality can be a tremendous source of affirmation, both for yourself and for the other. It can provide a sense of security, physical safety, and joyful expectation. It can be part of a new creation.

But to be honest, it has all too often been instead a source of pain, abuse, confusion, injury, infection, and even death.

Clearly, sexuality was designed to be an original blessing to us from God. Yet, it seems overly affected by peer pressure and a desire to belong. Sex is capable of granting a temporary respite from loneliness if it is used in a casual or destructive manner. But the respite is temporary; loneliness will return—perhaps with an eroding sense of self-esteem.

Sexuality may survive with little or no spiritual nurture, with casual use or with careless choice. But sexuality thrives on careful discernment, spiritual affirmation, loving commitment, and a sense of awe and wonder.

Those who use the gift of sexuality in the way God intended are willing to forego its promise of instant but shallow intimacy and seek to build a trusting, loving, and committed relationship as its foundation.

Sexuality offers us many choices over the course of our lifetime—many of them are difficult, complex, and have life-changing results. All around us are those who are willing to tell us how this gift can be used, should be used, must be used.

Yet it is our knowledge that this is a good gift from God that is important in our decision-making. It is designed for giving and receiving pleasure in an intimate and loving relationship, a gift that may be used to bring another life into the world, a gift that has great power and mystery.

We must each pray through, think through, and talk through our decisions about this powerful gift for ourselves. Scripture, tradition, reason, and our own experience—these are important sources for discovering what the gift of sexuality means to each of us. Ask for God's guidance; talk with someone whose life and faith you respect; don't substitute feelings for facts. Honor this great gift by seeking to know and understand its place in your life and in the lives of others.

May the gift of sexuality be a blessing in your life and a blessing to God, Creator of all gifts.

Points of Departure

Δ *Thoughts to Ponder*

> Remember that your sexual self is a good gift of God. Treat it that way.

> You are much, much more than just a sexual being.

> Be careful. You live in a world with unprecedented sexual freedom and unprecedented sexual responsibility.

> Casual sex erodes self-esteem and diminishes this gift of God. If you know anyone who gives their gift of sexuality away easily, you know how damaging it can be.

> Be pro-active about your sexuality, not re-active. Think things through for yourself ahead of time so you won't find yourself simply reacting to a situation. Talk with a person whose faith you admire. They'll be able to help you think it through.

> If you are or have been the victim of date rape, sexual abuse, rape, or incest, get some help. Your campus minister, dorm supervisor, or college health center will know what is available.

> If you know someone who is the victim of date rape, sexual abuse, rape, or incest, help that person get help.

> Ignorance is definitely not bliss, nor is it something to be embarrassed about. Get information, get help, find out.

> Always remember you are a child of God. God loves you.
—Thomas C. Ettinger

Δ Time is one of the most neglected topics in discussions of human relations. It takes a long time to make a soul. It takes a long time to make love. Intimacy takes time.
—From *Soul Making* by Alan W. Jones

Δ Do not open your heart to everyone, but discuss your private concerns with a person who is wise and who reveres God.
—From *The Imitation of Christ* by Thomas à Kempis

Δ Even in the Bible we have the Song of Songs; and really one can imagine no more ardent, passionate, sensual love than is portrayed there (see 7:6). It's a good thing that the book is in the Bible, in face of all those who believe that the restraint of passion is Christian (where is there such restraint in the Old Testament?).

—From *Letters and Papers from Prison* by Dietrich Bonhoeffer

Δ Contrary to Mrs. Grundy, sex is not sin. Contrary to Hugh Hefner, it's not salvation either. Like nitroglycerin, it can be used either to blow up bridges or heal hearts.

—From *Wishful Thinking* by Frederick Buechner

Journaling: Ideas for Written Reflection

Have you ever been in a situation when you felt pressured sexually? What did you do? Take time to reflect on what you might do the next time you are under pressure. Ask friends, family, or your campus minister for help thinking this through.

Prayers: For the World, for Others, for Myself

THE TYRANNY OF GRADES:
Measuring Yourself

Opening Prayer

Graceful God, remind me to be gentle toward myself. Amen.

Scripture Focus

The Lord is merciful and gracious. (Psalm 103:8)

Daily Scripture Readings

Sunday	1 Corinthians 12:4-11
Monday	John 1:14-18
Tuesday	Romans 12:3-8
Wednesday	Exodus 3:1-12
Thursday	James 3:13-18
Friday	Joel 2:12-13
Saturday	Galatians 5:22-26

The Focus for Reflection

The tyranny of grades, of making it, of doing well. Sometimes, in academia as well as in football, it turns out that winning isn't everything—it's the only thing.

The examples are rampant. Last year, someone stole a copy of the test used to accredit physicians. Last month, another famous historian was uncovered as a plagiarist. Last week, the honor board at a prestigious university expelled a dozen students for cheating on final exams. The number of suicides—many the result of academic pressure—among young people is alarmingly high and growing.

And, frighteningly enough, the pressure is understandable. It's there—from parents, peers, professors. The pressure to make the grade, to make the team, to make it into the finals is very, very real.

It's one way—an insidious way—of measuring yourself against others.

Don't get the wrong impression. Grades are important—but so is learning on the way to getting the grade. Doing your best is important—but so is not doing yourself in as you strive for your best.

So, in addition to grades and fraternity or sorority memberships and where you finish in the triathalon, you'd better come up with some additional ways to measure yourself, to keep track of your studies, to define who you are.

Grace is another way to measure yourself. The measure of God's grace. Lavished upon you, according to the Gospel of John. God's grace, the word that because you are a child of God, you are accepted and loved—this is the real measure of who you are.

When you have done your best, when you have run the race as well as you can, God's grace meets you, takes your measure and finds that you are God's own—beloved, holy, God's son or daughter. A member of the family of God.

Jimmy Cliff, a reggae artist from the Caribbean, says it well in his song "Brightest Star." He sings about the world of competition and everyone's need for recognition. At bottom, he says, there's no need to pretend to be what you're not. Instead, he says, just be yourself, because everyone plays their own part in life, so "Make sure you play yours from the heart."

Play it from the heart. Whether it's grades or athletics or relationships, play it from the heart.

Because at some point in the future, failure lurks. Human limitation will visit without warning. That inevitability is impossible to deny—especially after mid-terms, on the way toward Christmas finals.

But those claims—of failure, of limits, even of death—are not the ultimate claims. Grace is the ultimate claim. Grace is the ultimate measure. Grace. Pure and simple.

Points of Departure

Δ Most of us judge ourselves on this false relativistic basis. If we meet someone richer, we feel poor; someone handsomer, we feel ugly; someone more fluent, we feel tongue-tied. If they are up, we are down. . . .

But human society is not a pulley system. Each person has his own value . . . own place . . . own distinctive gifts and limitations. A pretty woman is no less pretty because a beautiful one enters the room; I am no poorer because I am lunching with a millionaire. My own writing does not become despicable when I am reading Shakespeare.

—From *The Best of Sydney J. Harris*

Δ One important direction in which to exercise gentleness is with respect to ourselves, never growing irritated with one's self or one's imperfections; for although it is but reasonable that we should be displeased and grieved at our own faults, yet ought we to guard against a bitter, angry, or peevish feeling about them.
—From *Introduction to the Devout Life* by St. Francis de Sales

Δ From time to time we fall flat on our faces! This is routine in soul making. . . .

We make mistakes, and thank God we do! In these "mistakes" lie our greatest hope for movement and change.
—From *Soul Making* by Alan W. Jones

Journaling: Ideas for Written Reflection
What do grades really say about who you are? Do you find it hard to keep grades and other measures of who you are—your body, your friends, your dates—in perspective?

Prayers: For the World, for Others, for Myself

TROUBLE, TEMPTATION, AND OTHER TRYING TIMES

Opening Prayer

Hold me fast and show me your path. Amen.

Scripture Focus

As your days, so is your strength.
(Deuteronomy 33:25)

Daily Scripture Readings

Sunday	Romans 8:31-39
Monday	Matthew 22:15-22
Tuesday	2 Samuel 22:32-37
Wednesday	Isaiah 35:3-11
Thursday	2 Corinthians 1:8-11
Friday	Psalm 46:1-3
Saturday	Matthew 6:13

The Focus for Reflection

It seems like an odd beginning for Jesus' public ministry, but this is the way the scriptures record it:

In those days Jesus came from Nazareth of Galilee and was baptized by John in the Jordan. And just as he was coming up out of the water, he saw the heavens torn apart and the Spirit descending like a dove on him. And a voice came from heaven, "You are my Son, the Beloved; with you I am well pleased."

> And the Spirit immediately drove him out into
> the wilderness. He was in the wilderness forty
> days, tempted by Satan; and he was with the
> wild beasts; and the angels waited on him.
>
> > (Mark 1:9-13)

Strange, isn't it? One moment Jesus is
baptized with the assurance that he is God's
beloved Son. The next moment, this same Jesus is
driven out into the wilderness and tempted for
forty days. First a baptism, a confession of faith,
and then trying times.

A life of faith is often like that—moments of
certainty followed right on the heels by
temptation and trouble.

Sometimes, when temptation comes, you may
well know what to do, which path to choose,
what action to take. You may be faced with a
straightforward decision between right and
wrong (plagiarizing, taking advantage of
someone else's knowledge on an exam, lying
about your responsibility for some action), and
still be tempted to choose the wrong. St.
Augustine, our ancestor in the faith, put it this
way: "Give me chastity and continence but not
yet."

Sometimes, when temptation comes, the way
through it may not be all that clear. Sometimes
there are no good options, but only the choice
between the lesser of two evils—deciding where
to come down on an issue that's not clearly black
or white, but some confusing shade of gray. Or,
choosing between the better of two "goods."
Those kinds of temptations call for discernment—

a way of working your way through to the best decision.

And what about the times that are neither blatant or subtle—the times that are just plain vexing? What about the Monday that turns out to be that terrible, horrible, no good, very bad day? Or the school term plagued by one disaster after another?

No matter how troubling your day—or your life—God's promise is sure and trustworthy: In the middle of it all God is there, giving strength, light, guidance, and companionship. You are not alone. God never gives up.

Whether God appears to you in the face of a friend, the comfort of the scriptures, or the quiet assurance of yet another day dawning, remember these words: "I am convinced that [nothing] . . . will be able to separate us from the love of God in Christ Jesus our Lord" (Romans 8:38-39).

Thanks be to God.

Points of Departure

Δ When you are tempted, seek advice often, and never deal harshly with others who are tempted; instead, comfort them as you would have them comfort you.
—From *The Imitation of Christ* by Thomas à Kempis

Δ What can I advise you to in the present case? in this trying hour? I would really advise you to sit still for a little while.
—John Wesley

Δ Don't forget, to be tempted, Jesus had at least to be interested in the temptation. Otherwise, it wasn't truly temptation.
—Thomas C. Ettinger

Δ I know all kinds of people who can't manage their lives because they are always thinking of the [whole thing]. They try to carry tomorrow's burdens with today's strength, and the burden proves too much for them and they break down. If, taking our Lord's advice, they would allow one day's troubles to be enough for the day, they could win through to nightfall. The psalmist put it clearly, "As thy days, so shall thy strength be." Troubles come one day at a time, and that is how strength is given and received.
—From *A Lover's Quarrel with the World* by R. Maurice Boyd

Δ Lord Jesus Christ,
You were poor
and in distress, a captive and forsaken as I am.
You know all [humanity's] troubles;
You abide with me
when all [others] fail me;
You remember and seek me;
It is your will that I should know you
and turn to you.
Lord, I hear your call and follow;
Help me.
—From *Letters and Papers from Prison* by Dietrich Bonhoeffer

Journaling: Ideas for Written Reflection

What's your relationship with God like when it comes to trouble and temptation? Can you call on God when times are tough? Can you be honest with God about who you are and what tempts you away from a close relationship with God?

Prayers: For the World, for Others, for Myself

THE POWER OF GRATITUDE

Opening Prayer
   With a heart full of thanks, I turn my eyes toward you, Great Giver of Life and Love. Amen.

Scripture Focus
   Thanks be to God for [the] indescribable gift! (2 Corinthians 9:15)

Daily Scripture Readings

Sunday	Psalm 95
Monday	Luke 17:11-19
Tuesday	Philippians 1:3-11
Wednesday	Psalm 100
Thursday	Luke 8:26-39
Friday	1 Thessalonians 5:16-18
Saturday	James 1:16-18

The Focus for Reflection

   It comes between *gratis* (free, for nothing) and *gratuitous* (unearned) in the dictionary. It's what your parents always made you say whenever anybody gave or did anything for you. And it's what you expressed, in note after endless note, for all the graduation gifts you received last spring.
   Gratitude. Urged by parents, dictated by social custom, or spoken straight from the heart, gratitude is a powerful force.

Webster's defines gratitude as "an awareness," and that's precisely what it is. An awareness of life as gift—all the big things and all the little things and all the things in between. Unearned. Freely given. No charge to the receiver.

Though we sometimes forget, it is easy to be grateful when things in life go well—good weather, good marks on the exam, a good class schedule for winter term. It's when things don't go so well that gratitude is tougher.

And yet, gratitude—in good circumstances or bad—has great transformational power. To say "thank you," to practice gratitude for life even amid its pain and discomfort and stress, is to recognize life for what it is—a gift from God. And this recognition, this awareness, is one of the most powerful forces in the world, because it affirms life, it affirms the present, it puts you in right relationship with the world.

Jesus lived a life of practiced gratitude. He encouraged others to do the same.

This week, let your faith encourage an awareness of life as gift in you. Be grateful. Say thank you. Practice gracious acceptance of life— all of it.

There will be times this week when gratitude is easy, when "thank you" comes naturally. There will be other times when you find you must force gratitude. Say thank you. Say thank you again and again. Say thank you when you don't feel especially grateful. Eventually, the power of gratitude will take over and a true awareness of life (in all its circumstances) as gift will begin.

Points of Departure

Δ Gratitude can help bring us to a point of surrender. It can change the energy in us and our environment. Gratitude diminishes the power of the problem and empowers the solution. It releases us from the tight, negative grasp of our present circumstance. It releases fear. It helps us move out and move forward. It breeds acceptance, the magic that helps us and our circumstances change.
—From *Codependents' Guide to the Twelve Steps* by Melody Beattie

Δ Thou that hast given so much to me,
Give one thing more—a grateful heart.
—George Herbert

Δ Gratitude is the rosemary of the heart.
—Minna Antrim

Δ O most high, Almighty, good Lord God,
        to you belong praise, glory, honour,
        and all blessing!
    Praised be my Lord God for all [God's]
        creatures, especially for our brother
        the sun. . . .
    Praised be my Lord for our sister the
        moon. . . .
    Praised be my Lord for our brother
        the wind. . . .
    Praised be my Lord for our sister water. . . .

Praised be my Lord for our brother fire. . . .
Praised be my Lord for our mother the earth,
    who sustains us and keeps us and
    brings forth various fruits and flowers
    of many colours, and grass.
—From "Canticle of the Sun" by St. Francis of Assisi

Journaling: Ideas for Written Reflection

Who is the most thankful person you know? Who among your friends greets life with a grateful attitude? Which of the people you know says "thank you" most often? How do you feel when you are around that person?

Who is the least thankful person you know? Who among your friends is least likely to greet life with a grateful attitude? How do you feel when you are around that person?

Prayers: For the World, for Others, for Myself

FINDING GOD IN SOLITUDE AND QUIET

Opening Prayer

Quiet and gentle Spirit, enfold me now with the healing power of solitude. Still my body, quiet my soul. Let me rest, for now, in you. Amen.

Scripture Focus

Be still, and know that I am God! (Psalm 46:10)

Daily Scripture Reading

Sunday	Psalm 46
Monday	Matthew 6:5-6
Tuesday	Lamentations 3:22-27
Wednesday	Mark 6:30-32, 45-47
Thursday	Isaiah 30:15-18
Friday	Luke 2:15-20
Saturday	Psalm 23

The Focus for Reflection

"Inside yourself, you shouldn't be running all the time." That's Tina Turner, rock superstar, quoting a Trappist monk. Both Turner, a practicing Buddhist, and the monk, a practicing Catholic, had one very basic belief in common: It takes time and solitude and a sense of quiet in order to know God.

"Be still, and know that I am God." A simple verse from the Bible, yet it is one of the hardest to follow.

When was the last time you sat still—perfectly still—for any length of time? Not just your body, but your mind? It's harder than it sounds . . . harder than it looks . . . and more rewarding than you could ever imagine.

God reaches out to each of us, all the time—through other people, through circumstance, and in that "still small voice." Most of the time, though, we're so busy, so active, so preoccupied that we don't hear what God is trying to say.

That's why quiet and solitude are such an important part of the life of faith. It is in solitude and silence that God waits for you. The more often you practice solitude, the more often you will find the God who waits, and the more often you will hear the God who speaks.

To quiet the body, to quiet the mind, to sit still and do nothing. Author Robert Fulghum senses the power of sitting still. In fact, he humorously suggests that a new religion could be based on this act. To belong would involve simply sitting still for fifteen minutes a day. "Amazing things might happen if enough people did this on a regular basis," he says. "Every chair, park bench, and sofa would become a church."

Quiet the body. Quiet the mind. Be still. Amazing things might happen. Just try it and see.

Points of Departure

Δ There is a sacred simplicity in not doing
something—and not doing it well. All the great
religious leaders have done it. The Buddha sat
still under a tree. Jesus sat still in a garden.
Muhammad sat still in a cave. And Gandhi and
King and thousands of others have brought
sitting still to perfection as a powerful tool of
social change. Passive resistance, meditation,
prayer—one and the same.

It works even with little kids. Instead of
telling them to sit still, you yourself can sit very
still and quiet. Before long they will pay a great
deal of attention to you. Students in class are also
thrown by silent stillness on the part of a teacher.
It is sometimes taken for great wisdom.

—From *It Was on Fire When I Lay Down on It* by Robert
Fulghum

Δ How good it is to center down!
    To sit quietly and see one's self pass by!
    The streets of our minds seethe with endless
        traffic;
    Our spirits resound with clashings, with noisy
        silences,
    While something deep within hungers and
        thirsts for the still moment and the resting
        lull.

—From *Meditations of the Heart* by Howard Thurman

Δ Certain springs are tapped only when we are alone.

—From *Gift from the Sea* by Anne Morrow Lindbergh

Journaling: Ideas for Written Reflection

Think back to a time when you were "bruised and fatigued" from too much contact with people. Where did you go for solitude and quiet? How much time did you spend alone? How did it feel to be by yourself? Did you come back from your solitude refreshed?

Prayers: For the World, for Others, for Myself

FINDING GOD AMID THE NOISE AND PRESSURE

Opening Prayer
Let me hear your quiet voice in the noises of this day. Amen.

Scripture Focus
O God of our salvation . . . You silence the roaring of the seas, the roaring of their waves, the tumult of the peoples. . . . You make the gateways of the morning and evening shout for joy. (Psalm 65:5, 7-8)

Daily Scripture Readings
Sunday	Psalm 107:28-31
Monday	Matthew 8:23-27
Tuesday	Exodus 19:16-21
Wednesday	John 6:16-21
Thursday	Daniel 3:19-30
Friday	Luke 19:28-40
Saturday	1 Chronicles 15:25-28

The Focus for Reflection

We seem to be running all the time. The notion of settling into a quiet place and being reflective is a good one, an important one—but some days life just doesn't happen that way.

Sometimes, the noise and the pressure don't— or won't—go away, even for a little while. Take the whole idea of having Advent in the middle of final exams and papers. Amid all that pressure, how do you find time for God? Or, take the living arrangement at college itself—whether it's your parents' home, a dorm room, or a shared apartment, likely as not the reverberating bass of street music or the hard-driving lyrics of Roxette will be pumping into your brain from the next-door neighbor's stereo, whether it's prayer or study you're trying to focus on.

In the middle of all that noise, how do you find space for God?

Oddly enough, the only place to find God in the middle of all the noise and pressure is just that—in the middle of all the noise and pressure.

Sometimes God's peace and serenity will elude you. Sometimes you will elude the peace and serenity God gives. When that happens, remember that God is, somehow, still there in the middle of it all.

Points of Departure

Δ The Rule does not call us to heroic deeds. Instead St. Benedict is telling me that my way to God lies in the daily and the ordinary. If I cannot find God here and now, in my home and in my work, in my daily routine, in the things that I handle in the kitchen or in the office, then it is no good looking for [God] anywhere else.
—From *Living with Contradiction* by Esther de Waal

Δ Sometimes God is the noise behind the noise. That may not make a lot of sense, but run with it

for a while. Trust it. Live your way into it. In
yoga, they call it "relaxing into the tension of the
position."
—Helen R. Neinast

Δ There is no event so commonplace but that
God is present within it.
—From *Now and Then* by Frederick Buechner

Δ All the way to heaven is heaven.
—St. Catherine of Siena

Journaling: Ideas for Written Reflection
What is most distracting to you right now as
you try to study, as you try to pray? Can you
think of a way to make that "noise" part of your
study and meditation time? Can you give the
noise over to God and release it from your mind?

Prayers: For the World, for Others, for Myself

PEACEMAKING IN A VIOLENT WORLD

Opening Prayer
God, abide with me in peace, that I may live peacefully in the world. Amen.

Scripture Focus
Blessed are the peacemakers, for they shall be called children of God. (Matthew 5:9)

Daily Scripture Readings
Sunday	Romans 14:19
Monday	Psalm 34:14
Tuesday	Isaiah 32:17-20
Wednesday	James 3:13-18
Thursday	Ephesians 2:14
Friday	Colossians 3:12-17
Saturday	Daniel 10:18-19

The Focus for Reflection

Richard Rhodes, Pulitzer Prize winner for his 1987 book *The Making of the Atomic Bomb*, lost his mother to suicide when he was thirteen months old. It was the middle of the Depression. When he was ten, his father remarried. Richard's stepmother turned out to be as cruel as the worst of folklore-cruel stepmothers.

For two and a half years, Richard and his brother were abused—kicked, beaten, denied baths and showers, deliberately starved. In *A Hole in the World: An American Boyhood*, he writes, "I've often wondered how my brother and I survived with our capacity to love intact. I always come back to the same answer—strangers helped us."

Strangers helped them. In the face of cruelty, poverty, and abuse, strangers helped them. Rhodes goes on to say that doing nothing allows evil to happen. "Don't be a bystander," he says. "Do something."

Do something. In the Hebrew tradition, it is called *tikun olam,* the repair, the healing of the world. It is peacemaking. That may seem a tall order—to make peace, to repair the world. And it is a tall order. But it is the call God makes to you each and every day—to be a peacemaker, a healer, a repairer.

There are so many ways—little and big—to do that. The sensitivities, the skills, and the time God has graced you with will open to you many chances to do the things that make for peace. One day at a time. One small corner of the world at a time. One piece at a time. One peace at a time.

Points of Departure

Δ One day we must come to see that peace is not merely a distant goal that we must seek but a means by which we arrive at that goal.
—From *Where Do We Go from Here: Chaos or Community?* by Martin Luther King, Jr.

Δ Keep yourself at peace first, and then you will be able to bring peace to others. A person who is

at peace with himself [herself] does more good than someone who is very learned. A person beset by conflicting passions turns even good things into bad. . . . Someone who is good and peaceful, on the other hand, sees the good side of everything.
—From *The Imitation of Christ* by Thomas à Kempis

Δ The question we often ask ourselves is "What can one person do?" One person can do little— but one and one and one and one can do a great deal.
—From *The Authentic Person* by Sydney J. Harris

Δ Peace is not simply the absence of conflict or the capacity for indifference in the ordinary course of our lives. Peace is vital, green growing and abundant life. Peace is a kind of being and seeing that has the quality of a dance.
—From "The Coming of the Prince of Peace" in *Living Prayer*, Nov.-Dec. 1990, by Wendy M. Wright

Journaling: Ideas for Written Reflection
There are many ways to be a peacemaker. Reflect on one or two skills or gifts you have that you can use to heal the world, one piece at a time.

Prayers: For the World, for Others, for Myself

GOD WITH US:
The Gift of the Incarnation

Opening Prayer
Christ has come to dwell among us. Thank you, God, for this most amazing gift. Amen.

Scripture Focus
For a child has been born for us. (Isaiah 9:6)

Daily Scripture Readings

Sunday	Luke 2:1-20
Monday	Isaiah 9:2-7
Tuesday	John 4:23-26
Wednesday	Colossians 1:15-20
Thursday	Isaiah 53:1-6
Friday	John 6:35-40
Saturday	Philippians 2:5-7

The Focus for Reflection

Incarnation. It means to embody. When it's spelled with a capital "I" it means God, embodied in Jesus Christ. It's a wonderful, mysterious word—eleven letters, four syllables, hundreds of years of speculation about what it really might mean.

The rosy-cheeked baby in the crib, surrounded by whitewashed sheep, sweet fresh hay, and grand glorious angels. Madonna and child. Befuddled but adoring father. Shepherds and animals rapt in attendance. It's a nice picture. A popular Christmas cameo.

But it's not the Incarnation.

The Incarnation was not so pretty, so serene, so beatific. It was probably loud and messy and painful, the way most births are. But this birth was in a dirty barn, strewn with rough hay, the mother unattended by any midwife.

This incarnation was not an easy one. It was hard labor, a birth ripe with the intrigue of Herod seeking the death of the infant, the wise kings seeking to avoid Herod, and the slaughter of innocent children. God came down from heaven to earth in that labor and birth, and the baby that Mary held in her arms was the Resurrection and the Life.

To deny the messiness, the painful labor, the crude humanity of God's first incarnation into the world is to deny the messiness, the pain, the humanity of God's repeated incarnations into the world since that first one.

For God is born among us, day in and day out. "As you did it to one of the least of these . . . you did it to me" (Matt. 25:40). The naked. The sick. The stranger. Messy. Painful. Human. God incarnate, again and again and again.

As you look around you this Christmas, look carefully. See God incarnate. In your professors. In your classmates. In your family. In your roommate. Yes, in your roommate. Messy. Painful. Human. It is an amazing gift, to see God's face in so many forms.

Merry Christmas! Happy Incarnation!

Points of Departure

Δ Not forever can the Christ stay hidden inside of you, but he will be born into your open life—with labor and pain on your part, to be sure; but with the shock of joy as well. . . .

He will live visibly in your deeds and in your doings. . . . Your language will change. The people will look at you and see a new thing and demand its name, and you will say, "Jesus," and they will go away wondering still; but you will smile as any mother would.
—From *Ragman and Other Cries of Faith* by Walter Wangerin, Jr.

Δ Mindfulness is what the monastic life teaches us. It is such a very simple thing to walk through life with my hands open, my eyes open, listening, alive in all my five senses to God breaking in again and again on my daily life. If the incarnation means anything at all it means this, that God is reaching me through the material things in the world of [God's] creating. . . . The whole world is potentially a sacrament. For it is through the material things of [this] world that God chooses to reveal [God's] self. If this is so then I should handle those things with reverence and respect, with joy, with gratitude.
—From *Living with Contradiction* by Esther de Waal

Δ Incarnation means that all ground is holy ground because God not only made it but walked on it, ate and slept and worked and died on it.
—From *Wishful Thinking* by Frederick Buechner

Journaling: Ideas for Written Reflection

Mother Teresa of Calcutta says that she sees the face of Christ in the people with whom she works every day. What does it do to the way you relate to people in your life if you imagine meeting Christ each time you meet them? How does this notion of "incarnation" affect your relationships?

Prayers: For the World, for Others, for Myself

CLEARING THE SLATE:
The Gift of Forgiveness

Opening Prayer

Almighty and ever-loving God, may I have the courage to know my sin, the strength to see your grace, and the mercy to forgive others even as I am forgiven. Amen.

Scripture Focus

If a shepherd has a hundred sheep, and one of them has gone astray, does he not leave the ninety-nine on the mountains and go in search of the one that went astray? And if he finds it, truly I tell you, he rejoices over it more than over the ninety-nine that never went astray. (Matthew 18:12-13)

Daily Scripture Readings

Sunday	John 8:3-11
Monday	Jeremiah 31:31-34
Tuesday	Matthew 18:21-35
Wednesday	Psalm 32:1-7
Thursday	Luke 15:11-24
Friday	Colossians 2:12-17
Saturday	Luke 7:36-50

The Focus for Reflection

Oh, how I loved my grandpa. We had a very special connection. In the years since his death I discovered that, unlike any other family members, our relationship moved him to special heights of love and giving.

Perhaps the most humorous example of Grandpa's love was the evening my family was visiting in Boston and my grandmother had prepared "boiled dinner"—cabbage, carrots, potatoes, ham, and squash thrown into a pot and boiled until done. I could handle everything but the dreaded squash. I simply would not, could not eat it.

The adults insisted that I eat all my dinner, including the squash. Dinner for all but myself ended, the table cleared and the dishes cleaned (except for mine). It was me, my plate, and the squash left at the table. Eight years old, alone, facing my squash.

Suddenly, quietly into the room walked my grandpa, carrying something under his sweater, the old cardigan he often wore. He glanced around the entrance to the dining room, saw that the coast was clear, opened his sweater, leaned over me, and said, "If you eat your squash, I'll give you these."

There in his hand, partially hidden by his sweater, was a whole package of chocolate cream-filled cupcakes. He had decided to brave the considerable "slings and arrows" of the others in order to encourage, support, and love me.

That was grace.

He died when I was fourteen. I was devastated. The rumor was that he had been to church only two times in his adult life—once for his marriage and once for the marriage of his son. That was it, twice.

I had for many years been concerned for the soul of everyone who did not go to church regularly. (Busy, wasn't I?) I asked my church school teacher if my beloved grandfather was with God, and my church school teacher asked me if my grandfather was a Christian. I told him that I did not know—that Grandpa had not been to church very often. My teacher said, "Then he's probably going to hell."

I was confused, hurt, angry, and deeply troubled. I walked for a long time that day, and as the sun began to set, I started to jog, slowly building speed. I was running from something. Running from what? I do not know.

Darkness was closing in on me. The air was full of nighttime smells. A beautiful evening, a tragic day.

Then it happened. I stopped abruptly, my lungs fairly bursting from the running. The smell of jasmine from a nearby bush, pungent, striking, oh so fragrant, captured all my senses.

I knew in that moment what I wish the whole world could know. God, who loves and forgives far beyond any levels I can, loved and forgave my grandpa. My love that evening for my grandpa was but a shadow of the love God was sharing with him that very moment. That evening, God helped me see that my love was but a part of God's love given in a measure for the care and nurture of others. Even my grandpa. Maybe especially my grandpa.

That was grace.

Points of Departure

Δ About a quarter before nine, while he was describing the change which God works in the heart through faith in Christ, I felt my heart strangely warmed. I felt I did trust in Christ, Christ alone for salvation; and an assurance was given me that he had taken away *my* sins, even *mine*, and saved me from the law of sin and death.
—John Wesley *Journal* May 24, 1738

Δ It is time, then, for us to embrace this frail flesh of ours with love. If we want to be disciples and saints, we must claim and cherish our humanness. What was good enough for God to embrace must be good enough for us.
—From *A Tree Full of Angels* by Macrina Wiederkehr

Journaling: Ideas for Written Reflection
God's love is wide and forgiving. When is your love and forgiveness toward yourself narrow and self-punishing? What things have you been unable to forgive yourself for? What difference would it make in your life if you "embraced this frail flesh" and forgave yourself as God forgives you?

Prayers: For the World, for Others, for Myself

LOVING YOURSELF AS GOD LOVES YOU

Opening Prayer

Surround me with your love, Creator God.
Amen.

Scripture Focus

The Lord loves you . . . (Deuteronomy 7:8,
RSV)

Daily Scripture Readings

Sunday	Ephesians 5:1-2
Monday	Leviticus 19:18
Tuesday	Colossians 3:12-17
Wednesday	Micah 6:8
Thursday	Hebrews 4:14-16
Friday	Deuteronomy 7:6-11
Saturday	Proverbs 15:17

The Focus for Reflection

Sharing time with someone you love,
understanding what you are called to be, feeling
sunshine on a spring morning, relishing the
beauty of fresh snow.

A walk at dusk along the seashore, a good
meal shared with friends, a movie that lifts your
spirits and inspires you.

Stepping on crunchy fall leaves, experiencing
quiet time alone, hearing music that reverberates
in your head, reaching out to someone in need.

153

Dozing off in the park on a sunny Saturday afternoon, enjoying the colorful and rich smell of flowers, worshiping in a caring community of faith, relaxing in a warm bath at night.

Playing fetch with the dog, reading a book just for fun, visiting someplace new, reading a magazine with pictures that mesmerize, starting a new class you want to be in, sharing your money for a worthy cause, keeping the faith even in times of chaos.

Asking questions born of real doubt, being tempted and meeting the challenge, gaining a new friend for life, having the courage to see the pain of others, relishing a full night of rest and sleep.

Floating on a river, singing songs of praise, staying current with the news, seeking help when you need it, praying for direction, hungering and thirsting for rightness, costuming for Halloween, living in a spirit of thanksgiving.

Caring so much that sometimes it hurts, eating in a balanced and healthy way, forgiving others because they are human too. . . .

These are some of the ways God shows love for you. These are ways you can love yourself.

The life of faith isn't all hard work and nose-to-the-grindstone. Sometimes you just have to accept yourself as you are, celebrate your growth so far, and rejoice in the moment of life God gives you today.

Points of Departure

Δ When we find the courage to look within and discover what is really going on with us, when we accept who we are, including our darker side, we will find that what happens outside, around, and within us begins to change.
—From *Codependents' Guide to the Twelve Steps* by Melody Beattie

Δ Considering the number of different species on this planet, the chances of being born a human being are about one in two billion. Considering the number of sperm produced by a single mating experience, the particular sperm that resulted in you was one in several million, at least. What is most astounding of all, however, is the absence of human awareness over the phenomenal triumph over impossible odds that a single human being represents. Human beings have been able to comprehend everything in the world except their uniqueness. Perhaps it is just as well. If ever we begin to contemplate our own composite wonder, we will lose ourselves in celebration and have time for nothing else.
—From *Human Options* by Norman Cousins

Δ I thought of how each of us needs the healing of memories. It does not take many failures, rejections, losses, putdowns, until the memory is wounded. A black and blue memory becomes the filter for narrow and tentative imaginations on the present, blinding us to the future. The Spirit must cure such remembrance through a reconstituting acceptance. . . . the awareness that one is not forsaken or abandoned.

—From *The Province Beyond the River* by W. Paul Jones

Δ I am brought back once again to seeing how vital it is that I take respect for myself seriously. St. Benedict is often more gentle than I tend to be, tender and nurturing, ready with concessions and allowances when they are needed.

—From *Living with Contradiction* by Esther de Waal

Journaling: Ideas for Written Reflection

How can you take time each day this week to be gentle with yourself, to love yourself, to give yourself the gift of celebrating the uniqueness of your life on this earth?

What parts of yourself do you need to acknowledge and accept in order to love yourself the way God loves you?

Prayers: For the World, for Others, for Myself

SUCCESS AND FAILURE

Opening Prayer

Help me to handle whatever comes my way this week. Amen.

Scripture Focus

Strive first for the kingdom of God. (Matthew 6:33)

Daily Scripture Readings

Sunday	Acts 1:21-26
Monday	Colossians 3:1-4
Tuesday	Psalm 25:4-5
Wednesday	Acts 2:17-18
Thursday	Deuteronomy 31:6-8
Friday	Luke 22:31-34
Saturday	John 17:17

The Focus for Reflection

The sign was printed on each student's study carrel. It was printed in big, bold, black letters: "You cannot fail unless you give up trying."

The Vashti Training School in Thomasville, Georgia is a resident school for troubled adolescents. The sign encourages their students and defines the challenge . . . to quit is to fail; to keep trying is to succeed.

When you think of success and failure, lots of things come to mind. We'd like to define success and failure in slightly different terms.

Put success and failure in this context: God has given each of us the heart, mind, soul, and strength to offer a full and vibrant response to life. Our acceptance of this gift of God's grace is an essential part of success and failure.

To be a success is to begin any journey in life by remembering all that God has done to bring you to this particular place. Acknowledging God's purpose and direction for yourself is a steady way to find direction for setting goals for yourself.

The next step in success and failure is to keep at it. Always remember that God has given you a uniqueness unlike any other. Keep plugging away with all your being, and you will succeed no matter what the "results" look like.

Finally, be aware of the presence of God in both success and failure. When you successfully accomplish what you set out to do, congratulations, and thanks be to God. When you are unable to accomplish a goal and you feel like a failure, remember that God has gone before you, is there with you, and prepares to meet you in every circumstance.

In God's eyes, we are all students in our study carrels, with God urging us on in love: "You cannot fail unless you give up trying."

Points of Departure

Handling Disappointment

Δ Whatever happened to Justus? He's the man who lost the election to become the twelfth disciple. Two men, Matthias and Justus, were nominated to replace Judas. Matthias was chosen (Acts 1:21-26). Was Justus hurt or did he accept it gracefully? The scripture doesn't say, only that the other man was the choice.

I am sure Justus was disappointed. He was a follower of Jesus from the beginning. Surely to become one of the twelve would be an honor beyond measure; yet he was passed by.

What we do with our disappointments may be more important than how we handle success. We usually measure up to success, but can we measure up to failure, especially when our self-esteem is at stake? If we do, we are able to overcome an egotism that always has to win or be first or succeed.

—From *Why Do Mullet Jump?* by Gene Zimmerman

Δ As he [Brother Lawrence] proceeded in his work he continued his familiar conversation with his Maker, imploring [God's] grace, and offering to [God] all his actions.

When he had finished it he examined himself how he had discharged his duty; if he found well, he returned thanks to God; if otherwise, he asked pardon, and, without being discouraged, he set his mind right again, and continued his exercise

of the presence of God as if he had never deviated
from it.

—From *The Practice of the Presence of God* by Brother
Lawrence

Journaling: Ideas for Written Reflection

Is it harder for you to handle success or
failure? What might it mean for you to give both
your success and your failures over to God?

Prayers: For the World, for Others, for Myself

HARD TIMES:
Mourning and Being Comforted

Opening Prayer

All my sorrow, all my brokenness, my pain, my hurt, my disappointment I give to you, O Healing God. Amen.

Scripture Focus

Blessed are those who mourn, for they will be comforted. (Matthew 5:4)

Daily Scripture Readings

Sunday	Job 2:11-13
Monday	2 Corinthians 1:3-7
Tuesday	Isaiah 40:1-11, 31
Wednesday	Psalm 126
Thursday	John 11:17-44
Friday	Isaiah 61:1-4
Saturday	Jeremiah 31:10-14

The Focus for Reflection

When my younger brother died, I remember how much I hurt inside. It felt as though there was a bloody hole where my heart should have been. After the sharp wrench of pain and shock fell away, I remember a dull empty ache. And underneath the ache, I remember nothing at all—the numbness of death itself.

Friends came to me—to talk, to listen, to sit with me. I prayed, searched the Bible for words of comfort, got angry at God, wept, slept exhausted, and not at all.

I went back to my work; the dull ache and numbness went with me.

"Blessed are those who mourn. . . ." Jesus' words haunted me. The mourning part I was beginning to understand—how wrenching, how lonely, how terrifying it can be. Blessed? That part rang hollow. I felt no blessing in the middle of the pain. For a long, long time I felt no blessing and no comfort.

Then slowly, imperceptibly, something began to shift. I awoke in the morning and the ache was still there, but so was a little bit of energy. And the next week, the ache again, but a little more energy.

I read about suicide—my brother had killed himself. I stumbled across words—in books, in magazines, from the mouths of friends and of strangers—that slowly, slowly began to envelop my numbness, to surround the ache, to melt the sorrow frozen inside. Through it all, I kept praying for comfort.

Someone said that it is through our wounded areas that God enters. Quietly, God began to enter my wounded areas, to cleanse the wound and heal the pain. Slowly, quietly, comfort came.

I still miss him, terribly. Six years after my brother's death, I still sometimes sob in my sleep when I dream about him. But the mourning melts into comfort. God is there—for me, for my brother. The pain is, somehow, blessed and made holy.

It is mysterious, sad, and wondrous beyond words.

When you face sorrow—the death of a friend, the loss of a love, the disappointment of a friendship, months when everything seems to go wrong—the promise is there. The promise is sure. "Blessed are those who mourn, for they shall be comforted."

Points of Departure

Δ Never let anything so fill you with sorrow as to make you forget the joy of Christ Risen.
—Mother Teresa of Calcutta in *Something Beautiful for God* by Malcolm Muggeridge

Δ Give sorrow words: the grief that does not speak
  Whispers the o'er-fraught heart and bids it break.
—From *Macbeth* by William Shakespeare

Δ No one ever told me that grief felt so like fear. I am not afraid, but the sensation is like being afraid. The same fluttering in the stomach, the same restlessness, the yawning. I keep on swallowing.

At other times it feels like being mildly drunk, or concussed. There is a sort of invisible blanket between the world and me. I find it hard to take in what anyone says. Or perhaps, hard to want to take it in.
—From *A Grief Observed* by C.S. Lewis

Δ What appears to be desert, scorching sands,
       is really,
   if given proper attention,
   the beauty that heals my worn and weary and
       depleted soul.

   Suffering, death, absence, and pain are linked
       in a wreath of
   beauty that heals.
   —From "Beauty that Heals" by Phyllis Tyler-Wayman

Journaling: Ideas for Written Reflection

The Jews, our ancestors in the faith, go to a wall in Jerusalem that was once part of their ancient temple to pray and mourn. It is called the wailing wall. Mark one page of your journal "Wailing Wall." Spend some time in prayer, writing down things for which you mourn—personally, at school, in the world.

Can you remember a time when you mourned and were comforted or had the pain lessened? What were you mourning? In what form did comfort come—through a friend, something you read, the healing beauty of nature, words from scripture, a dream in the middle of the night?

What in your life, today, do you need to mourn? Who in your life, today, do you need to comfort?

Prayers: For the World, for Others, for Myself

GOD'S EXTRAVAGANT GRACE:
Surrounding You in Love

Opening Prayer

Help me to know the grace surrounding me.
Amen.

Scripture Focus

In the beginning was the Word. (John 1:1)

Daily Scripture Readings

Sunday	Psalm 23
Monday	2 Corinthians 5:16-21
Tuesday	Genesis 1:1, 31
Wednesday	John 3:16
Thursday	John 1:1-5
Friday	Nehemiah 9:6-15
Saturday	Psalm 59:10

The Focus for Reflection

Hindsight: understanding an event after it has
happened.

Hindsight is how I learn most things. At times
my hindsight is 20/20; at other times, it is less
than that.

My earliest memories of the Cape Island
Baptist Church in Cape May, New Jersey, are of
being a second grader in Miss Alice's class. I was
seven; she was seventy. She loved kids, and we
loved her.

I'll never forget her face because every time I saw her at church, that face was framed by a weasel stole. For the uninitiated, a weasel stole was a curious fur piece popular in the fifties, primarily with older women. The stole was made of two weasel skins, heads intact, sewn together, and draped over the shoulders. And there was Miss Alice, looking down at us from between those two weasels—their teeth bared, eyes glassy, staring.

In some odd sort of way, we were blessed to have Miss Alice and those weasels in our lives, because Miss Alice sat down with us kids, each and every Sunday, and taught us about God. God's love, God's care, God's call for each and every one of us. Through Miss Alice, weasels and all, I learned what it meant to be claimed as a child of God.

In hindsight, I see that Cape Island Baptist Church was blessed to have Miss Alice as a Sunday school teacher. In hindsight, I understand that Miss Alice was blessed to have that church as her spiritual home. In hindsight, that church stands as one of the most obvious examples of God's "prevenient grace" in my life.

God precedes us wherever we go. Dr. Maurice Boyd, in his book *A Lover's Quarrel with the World*, writes of the celebrated English lay preacher Hugh Redwood. Redwood was facing a particularly difficult time in his life—a time when it seemed that no matter how earnestly he prayed, he felt the guidance of the Lord was far from him.

One night, while sitting by the fire he happened to notice a Bible on the table by his chair. The Bible was open to Psalm 59. Redwood began to read and when he got to the tenth verse he found these words, "The God of my mercy shall prevent me."

The words Redwood read were from the King James Version of the Bible. To the modern reader, the word "prevent" means to keep something from happening. In 1611, in King James' English, the word *prevent* meant "to go before." Psalm 59:10 actually meant, "The God of my mercy shall go before me."

After reading that psalm, Redwood noticed that someone had written in the margin a paraphrase that he would never forget. "My God, in loving kindness, shall meet me at every corner." Powerful words. They spoke to Hugh Redwood that night. God was there. God's grace had preceded Redwood to that place, and God was waiting for him there.

All of us will face many corners in life. Some will be positive, welcomed, nurturing. Others will be devastating, stressful, spirit draining. All these corners will be transitions for us.

The corners of college will take you many places—places you could only imagine before. When you face a corner in life, take a moment and imagine, remind yourself, that God, in loving kindness, has promised to meet you at every corner.

That is prevenient grace. Thanks be to God.

Points of Departure

Δ Give what you command, and command what you will.
—From *Confessions* by St. Augustine

Δ How can I find God? That is like a bird asking, "How can I find the air?" or a fish asking, "How can I find the ocean?" We couldn't even think of finding God if [God] had not already found us!
—From *A Lover's Quarrel with the World* by R. Maurice Boyd

Δ We are not alone, we live in God's world.
    We believe in God. . . .
    We trust in God. . . .
    In life, in death, in life beyond death,
        God is with us.
    We are not alone.
    Thanks be to God. Amen.
—From A New Creed of The United Church of Canada

Journaling: Ideas for Written Reflection

In what ways do you see, in hindsight, that God has surrounded you in grace? What difference does it make to your faith if you believe that God is present at all times, even when you can't feel God's presence?

Prayers: For the World, for Others, for Myself

GOD'S EXTRAVAGANT GRACE:
Making Your Brokenness Whole

Opening Prayer

Draw me close to you, that I may know your healing grace. Amen.

Scripture Focus

Listen! I am standing at the door, knocking . . . (Revelation 3:20)

Scripture Readings

Sunday	Ephesians 2:1-10
Monday	Luke 23:42-43
Tuesday	Romans 5:20
Wednesday	Luke 15:11-24
Thursday	John 3:1-8
Friday	Psalm 42:1-2
Saturday	Revelation 3:20

The Focus for Reflection

If you've ever been in love, you've gotten a glimpse of what God's saving grace is all about. God's saving grace hits you the same way falling in love does; somewhere deep inside you something major shifts, and the pieces all fall into place. You are somehow never the same again.

The broken places heal; the pain is put into joyous perspective; and you understand life in a whole new way.

To know God's love, to be touched by God's justifying grace, is a life-shaking, life-changing, life-rearranging experience. Rather than putting your belief in yourself or in your parents or in the ways of the world, you discover for yourself that God is the way, the truth, and the life. God's grace envelops you, and for once you understand the world the way it was created to be—full, rich, at peace.

Created in you is an urgency, a need to know God, to follow in God's way, to trust that God is with you always.

Printer's jargon uses the word *justify* to mean setting type in a way that all lines are equal in length. Justification puts the printed lines in right relationship with each other. The religious sense of justification is very similar. It simply means being brought into right relationship—with God, with the world, with yourself.

There are as many ways to accept God's justifying grace as there are ways to fall in love. For some people, it happens all at once, "at first sight." For most, it is gradual and cumulative. Some people come to love eagerly; others drag their feet, kicking and screaming.

Whatever way you come to it, it doesn't matter much. The truth is that God reaches out to you with grace to make you a new creature in Christ.

Points of Departure

Δ Like any other gift, the gift of grace can be yours only if you'll reach out and take it. Maybe being able to reach out and take it is a gift, too.
—From *Wishful Thinking* by Frederick Buechner

Δ We come to Jesus in our own unique and idiosyncratic way. Temperament and timing have a lot to do with it.
—From *Soul Making* by Alan W. Jones

Δ You must picture me alone in that room in Magdalen, night after night, feeling, whenever my mind lifted even for a second from my work, the steady unrelenting approach of Him whom I so earnestly desired not to meet. That which I greatly feared had at last come upon me. In the Trinity Term of 1929 I gave in, and admitted that God was God, and knelt and prayed: perhaps, that night, the most dejected and reluctant convert in all England. I did not see then what is now the most shining and obvious thing; the Divine humility which will accept a convert even on such terms.
—From *Surprised by Joy* by C.S. Lewis

Δ Amazing grace! How sweet the sound
That saved a wretch like me!
I once was lost, but now am found;
Was blind, but now I see.
—John Newton

Journaling: Ideas for Written Reflection

How has God's justifying grace touched you? Can you identify ways—either specific times or gentle processes—in which God's grace has changed your life?

Prayers: For the World, for Others, for Myself

GOD'S EXTRAVAGANT GRACE:
Smoothing Out the Rough Edges

Opening Prayer
God, center me on you and your grace. Amen.

Scripture Focus
God's love has been poured into our hearts through the Holy Spirit. (Romans 5:5)

Daily Scripture Readings

Sunday	Hebrews 4:14-16
Monday	1 Peter 1:13-16
Tuesday	1 John 1:5-10
Wednesday	Ephesians 1:3-14
Thursday	2 Timothy 2:1-7
Friday	2 Corinthians 8:1-7
Saturday	Colossians 4:2-6

The Focus for Reflection

Prevenient grace is God meeting you at every corner. Justifying grace is reaching out to meet God's love, saying "Yes," and turning a corner in your faith journey. What comes next?

Smoothing out the rough edges. The theologians call it "sanctification," and it is a lifelong process, full of fits and starts along the way.

For John Wesley, God's smoothing grace, God's sanctifying grace, led to believers having hearts "habitually filled with the love of God and neighbor."

For you, it might mean coming to understand your life as more and more focused on living by faith. Instead of dabbling in the faith, you come to understand the faith as the hub, the center out of which you live. Little by little, God's grace uncovers more and more of God's image in you. It's the process of becoming a "new, improved version" of yourself, better able to love God, neighbor, and yourself.

As one forgiven, you become more forgiving. As one who is loved, you become more loving. As a healed one, you start to become a healer.

It is a slow process, sometimes painful, sometimes joyous, always one day at a time. But once you fall in love, once you turn the corner, once you set out on the road to sanctification, God's extravagant grace promises that there will be wonderful surprises along the way.

Points of Departure

Δ I go along perhaps for some days, and then suddenly it comes, as this evening climbing a hill, at the top the sea spread out before me . . . a sudden happiness possessing my heart, penetrating to each corner of my being, like an electric current, physical; all fear gone, burden of self lifted, nothing to dread, nothing to regret, complete trust in whatever has shaped my destiny and the destiny of all life. . . . I say. This is Grace.

—From *Like It Was: The Diaries of Malcolm Muggeridge*

Δ We hold that the wonder of God's acceptance and pardon does not end God's saving work, which continues to nurture our growth in grace. Through the power of the Holy Spirit we are enabled to increase in the knowledge and love of God and in love for our neighbor.

—From *The Book of Discipline of The United Methodist Church, 1988*

Δ Grace is the *re*union of life with life, the *re*conciliation of the self with itself. Grace is the acceptance of that which is rejected. Grace transforms fate into a meaningful destiny; it changes guilt into confidence and courage. There is something triumphant in the word "grace."

—From *The Shaking of the Foundations* by Paul Tillich

Journaling: Ideas for Written Reflection

As you grow deeper in the spiritual life, you notice new and different ways that God's love pours out of your life into the lives of others. Reflect on the way God's grace in your life has touched other persons' lives this week.

Prayers: For the World, for Others, for Myself

ANGER, FEAR, AND GUILT:
The Unholy Trinity

Opening Prayer

Accept me as I am, O gracious God—and help me to do the same. Amen.

Scripture Focus

And [Peter] went out and wept bitterly. (Luke 22:62)

Daily Scripture Readings

Sunday	Isaiah 35:3-4
Monday	Matthew 26:36-46
Tuesday	Psalm 27:1
Wednesday	Luke 22:54-62
Thursday	Mark 16:8
Friday	Psalm 109:1-12
Saturday	Mark 11:15-19

The Focus for Reflection

We experience lots of feelings. Some of them "feel" better than others.

Contrary to what we are taught, there are no "wrong" feelings. How we express our feelings may be cause to cringe, but the feelings themselves are not wrong. What we do with them is another question.

Fear, guilt, and anger . . . the Unholy Trinity. You'll find these three in your life often—whether you want to or not.

The first time I heard these three called the "Unholy Trinity" I was fascinated. The suggestion that fear, guilt, and anger might all be part of the same center was intriguing.

This concept may help you understand yourself better. Assume that whenever you feel one of the three—fear, anger, guilt—the other two are in some way present as well. It won't always be so, but it will be true ninety percent of the time. These feelings feed off each other and magnify each other.

For example, a friend confronts you about something you did (or didn't do) that you feel guilty about. You feel anger at yourself. You feel afraid you've hurt the relationship. Guilt, anger, and fear. The Unholy Trinity.

The next time one of these three raises its head in your heart, try this simple exercise. If you're angry, ask what you feel afraid of or guilty about. If you're afraid, ask what is making you angry or why you might be feeling guilt in relationship to what you're fearing. If you're feeling guilty, check for the presence of the other two.

Sometimes you might need help confronting the Unholy Trinity. If so, seek out a friend, a trusted professor, or your campus minister.

Doing this can help you sort through the tangled ball that feelings sometimes are. There is no avoiding feelings; feelings are just that—feelings. Thinking through what those feelings mean for you can be a real help, especially when confronting the Unholy Trinity.

Points of Departure

Δ When we repress a thought or feeling, we do not thereby get rid of it; for it inevitably takes its revenge by returning, far stronger, in a form that shocks us with its unexpected intensity.
—From *For the Time Being* by Sydney J. Harris

Δ What has most often opened my eyes to my own unconscious sin is the witness of friends when they have told me about their own faults. This, let it be noticed is the complete opposite of judgment. Instead of denouncing my guilt, they spoke to me of their own, and an amazing light flashed into the depths of my heart. An inward voice murmured, "This is true of myself, but I have never recognized it."
—From *Guilt and Grace* by Paul Tournier

Δ Our cultural definition of "helping" someone only involves being supportive. . . . Individuals are not socially conditioned to see anything constructive or helpful in engaging someone in an aggressive interaction by confronting them, getting angry at them, or facilitating the release of their angry feelings by letting them get angry in return.
—From *Creative Aggression* by George R. Bach and Herb Goldberg

Journaling: Ideas for Reflection

What do you do when you find yourself experiencing "bad" feelings? Who do you talk to about your guilt, fear, and anger?

Prayers: For the World, for Others, for Myself

REFLECTIONS ON FAITH

Opening Prayer
Strengthen my faith, God. Amen.

Scripture Focus
Now faith is the assurance of things hoped for, the conviction of things not seen. (Hebrews 11:1)

Daily Scripture Readings
Sunday	Hebrews 11:1-3; 12:1-2
Monday	Exodus 14:30-31
Tuesday	Luke 13:18-21
Wednesday	Jeremiah 31:3-6
Thursday	Mark 5:24-34
Friday	Genesis 15:1-6
Saturday	2 Chronicles 20:20-21

The Focus for Reflection

Blind faith. Simple faith. An act of faith. Keep the faith. Saved by faith. Walk by faith. The fruit of the Spirit is faith. Faith healing.

O ye of little faith. Faith without works is dead. My faith is shattered. I've lost faith in you.

Faith. A simple five-letter word—yet one so full of meanings and nuance that it defies definition.

Faith. One of those time-worn words, worn so thin that you're likely to walk right past it

without noticing, unless something or someone—
a particularly good or bad example—grabs your
attention.

The biblical Hebrew language lacks a noun
equivalent to our English word *faith*. For the
ancient Hebrews, faith wasn't a matter of whether
or not to believe in the existence of God. The
Israelites took this for granted. The issue of faith
was whether to acknowledge this God as Savior
and Lord, to trust this God, and to commit their
lives to God and to God's laws.

By all accounts of the exodus tradition, faith
was not a one-time, static condition of life, but a
dynamic activity of the mind, heart and will . . . a
day-by-day response to the grace of God.

In the New Testament, Jesus showed the same
faith and trust in God that ancient Israel did. For
him, the opposite of faith was not disbelief, but
worry. In the Book of Mark, when the disciples
woke Jesus with their anxious cries during the
storm at sea, Jesus asked them, "Why are you
afraid? Have you no faith?" Why are you
worried, friends?

When we replace worry with faith, the Bible
says we become "new creations." Faith works
itself out in the form of love for God and for
others, and in hope and trust for the future.

There will be times, of course, when faith can
show itself only as hoping against hope. That was
true in biblical times; it's also true in college and
university times. There will be people, events,
and coursework that will challenge your faith,
shake it, maybe even threaten to shatter it. Do not
fear the questions. Faith can grow through

doubts.

But remember—the opposite of faith is not doubt—it's worry. With all the new information and experiences buzzing around inside your head, know that faith is still possible because it lives and grows and changes. Faith carries with it an aura of mystery that beckons you on. Listen for that mystery in your studies, in your relationships, in your mind, and in your heart.

Points of Departure

Δ It is an overwhelming experience to fall into the hands of the living God, to be invaded to the depths of one's being by [God's] presence, to be, without warning, wholly uprooted from all earth-born securities and assurances.
—From *A Testament of Devotion* by Thomas R. Kelly

Δ I shall never believe that God plays dice with the world.
—Albert Einstein

Δ I believe that God can and will bring good out of evil, even out of the greatest evil. For that purpose [God] needs [those] who make the best use of everything. I believe that God will give us all the strength we need to help us to resist in all time of distress. But [God] never gives it in advance, lest we should rely on ourselves and not on [God] alone.
—From *Letters and Papers from Prison* by Dietrich Bonhoeffer

Δ Anyone not about to kill himself [or herself] lives by faith. It is what keeps us going when love has turned to hate or hope to despair. Faith carries us forward when there is no longer reason to carry on.

—From *Life Maps* by Jim Fowler and Sam Keen

Journaling: Ideas for Written Reflection

If worry is the opposite of faith, what issues this week are testing grounds for your faith? If faith is a day-by-day response to God, in what areas of your life are you responding in faith?

Prayers: For the World, for Others, for Myself

REFLECTIONS ON HOPE

Opening Prayer

O God, in you I live and move and have my being. Fill me with hope and joy this week. Amen.

Scripture Focus

For I am convinced that [nothing] in all creation, will be able to separate us from the love of God in Christ Jesus our Lord. (Romans 8:38-39)

Daily Scripture Readings

Sunday	1 Thessalonians 5:8
Monday	Romans 8:31-39
Tuesday	Galatians 5:5
Wednesday	Romans 15:13
Thursday	Psalm 39:7
Friday	Romans 5:1-5
Saturday	Ephesians 4:4-6

The Focus for Reflection

There are more than eighty references to it in the Bible. *The United Methodist Hymnal* lists 130 songs about it. *Bartlett's Familiar Quotations* refers to it more than 120 times. *The Quotable Woman* notes it in no less than 30 citations.

"It" is hope. One of the "big three" in the Christian tradition—faith, hope, love. Poets have written about it, lovers have practiced it, revolutions have been born of it. Yet hope is still, sometimes, elusive and fleeting.

Hope isn't the same as optimism, for optimism is at least in part based on an assessment of life's situation, while hope is somewhat more blind and more stubborn in the face of disappointments and setbacks.

Hope isn't the same as wishing, because hope is more steadfast, more faithful, more long-lived than merely wishing things to be different.

Hope isn't the same as a positive outlook, because hope weathers storms that drive a positive outlook out to sea.

Hope sometimes involves waiting, yet it is possible to wait without hope. Waiting with hope is a different sort of thing altogether. It is an affirmation that God—not you or I—is in charge, and that God is faithful, worthy of our hope.

First Peter, written to Christians in the northern part of Asia Minor who were undergoing intense persecution and even crucifixion, is called the "Letter of Hope." Throughout this short letter are words of hope, earnestly written.

There is assurance: "The word of the Lord endures forever" (1:25).

There is encouragement: "You are . . . a royal priesthood, a holy nation, God's own people" (2:9).

There are promises: "By [God's] great mercy we have been born anew to a living hope through the resurrection of Jesus Christ" (1:3, RSV).

There is exhortation: "Prepare your minds . . . set all your hope on the grace that Jesus Christ will bring you" (1:13).

Memory looks backward. Hope looks forward. Hope is the memory of God's love and grace, alive somehow—like a flower growing through a crack in the sidewalk (sometimes only God knows how)—in the future.

As you face your future, today, tomorrow, next week, next semester, hold fast to this blessing of the Christian faith:

May the God of hope fill you with all joy and peace in believing, so that you may abound in hope by the power of the Holy Spirit. (Romans 15:13)

Points of Departure

Δ In a sense, it [suicide] is an intensely religious subject, because it has to do with our attitude toward ourselves, God, and the value of human life.There could hardly be a subject more directly related to the trinity of faith, hope, and love, because when a person chooses suicide, he or she apparently feels that there is no reason for faith, no hope, and no one who loves.
—From "Soul at the End of Its Rope" by J. Ellsworth Kalas

Δ The kind of hope I often think about (especially in situations that are particularly hopeless, such as prison) I understand above all as a state of mind, not a state of the world. Either we have hope within us or we don't; it is a

dimension of the soul, and it's not essentially dependent on some particular observation of the world or estimate of the situation.
—From *Disturbing the Peace* by Václav Havel

Δ "Hope" is the thing with feathers—
    That perches in the soul—
    And sings the tune without the words—
    And never stops—at all—
    —Emily Dickinson

Δ We need images of hope to counteract our horror, knowledge of grace to counteract our knowledge of sin. . . . But in my spiritual life I have learned that hope and grace do not come cheap. They require honest self-scrutiny first, and then confession, an offering up of our own inner darkness to the source of forgiveness and transformation.
—From *To Know As We Are Known* by Parker J. Palmer

Journaling: Ideas for Written Reflection
    What does it mean to you to "hope" for something? Does it involve prayer, waiting, activity, dreaming? What are your deepest hopes for your life right now?

Prayers: For the World, for Others, for Myself

REFLECTIONS ON LOVE

Opening Prayer
God of love, enfold me in your arms. Amen.

Scripture Focus
Love is from God. (1 John 4:7)

Daily Scripture Readings

Sunday	1 Corinthians 13
Monday	Deuteronomy 6:5
Tuesday	Matthew 5:38-48
Wednesday	1 Peter 4:8
Thursday	Song of Solomon 8:6-7
Friday	1 John 4:7-12
Saturday	1 Corinthians 14:1

The Focus for Reflection

I had known him for many years. An honest, fair, and caring man. After more than thirty years, his marriage had ended in divorce. His career as a professor of political science had taken him into many situations where his basic appreciation of people had stood the test of time.

I had always seen him as a very loving man, capable of both affection and friendship. We had the chance to share a meal recently, and out of the blue he asked, "What is love?"

Tough question.

We talked easily of our love for pizza, ice cream, and football. We talked more carefully of our love for the arts, history, and our heroes. With some hesitation we referenced love of parents—his dead, mine still living. We noted differences between love of others and the love one feels for another that includes a sexual attraction.

As we talked we found much common ground. And yet, we both knew we were circling a great truth, but it was like sand slipping through our fingers.

Finally, I told him that whenever I think about love I think not whether I can touch, see, taste, or hear love; rather I think of God's love for each of us, the many people I have loved through the years, the many from whom I have felt love, and the challenge to love that God puts before us to love even those who do not love us.

My friend nodded and smiled. I felt, in that moment, we both knew that it was love for each other that had brought us to this time and place and that would ease our struggle as we sought to love God, ourselves, and others.

Points of Departure

Δ One of the hardest transitions to make in the life of faith is that from loving someone for our own sake and loving someone for his or her own. One of the fundamental questions posed by the tradition of the mystics is, "How far do I love God for my own sake and how far for [God's]?"
—From *Soul Making* by Alan W. Jones

Δ Love is a great thing, a great good in every way, for it alone lightens every burden and passes smoothly over all misfortunes. . . . The noble love of Jesus spurs us on to do great things.
—From *The Imitation of Christ* by Thomas à Kempis

Δ What distinguishes God from mere humans is not the power to thunder or coerce, but the power to overcome fury by unfailing love. . . . Long after we have given up loving, God loves on.
—From *The Divine Passion* by Robert G. Hamerton-Kelly

Δ If I take one of the difficult people and mentally give myself to that person, something is bound to happen. By an exercise of the imagination, I picture myself with that person on a desert island waiting for the turn of the tide, or sheltered in a mountain hut while a storm rages. To survive, each one of us must come to the other's aid. In discovering ourselves as we really are, in the urgency that has been forced upon us, we make room for love to happen.
—From *A Book of Hours* by Elizabeth Yates

Journaling: Ideas for Written Reflection
Love is a very strong feeling. It's also a way of relating to others, even when you don't "feel" love. Knowing this, what might it mean for you to "make love your aim" this week?

Prayers: For the World, for Others, for Myself

BLESSED TO BE A BLESSING:
Sacrifice and Servant Leadership

Opening Prayer
Use my gifts, servant God. Amen.

Scripture Focus
[Christ Jesus] emptied himself, taking the form of a slave. (Philippians 2:7)

Daily Scripture Readings

Sunday	1 Corinthians 12:1-31
Monday	2 Chronicles 1:7-13
Tuesday	3 John 5-8
Wednesday	Isaiah 42:1-9
Thursday	1 Peter 4:9-11
Friday	Matthew 25:31-46
Saturday	Philippians 2:5-11

The Focus for Reflection

In Hermann Hesse's story *Journey to the East*, a band of men sets out on a mythical journey. The central figure is Leo, the servant who accompanies the party. He does their menial chores, but he also sustains them with his spirit and his song. He is, according to the story, a person of great spirit. When Leo disappears, the group falls into disarray, and they abandon the journey.

The narrator, one of the band of men, after some years of wandering finds Leo and is taken into the Order that had sponsored the journey. He discovers there that Leo, whom he had known first as a servant, was in fact the head of the Order, its guiding spirit, a great and noble leader.

The idea of servant-leader is an old one. In the Bible, Jesus talks about how those who would be first will be last, and those who would be last will be first. He himself, shortly before his death, picks up a towel and, acting as a servant, washes the feet of his disciples. It is shocking to some of them, yet he insists on washing each one's feet. It is a gift of service.

That gift of service is the same one to which we, as Christians, are called. Like the disciples, we must lose our lives in order to find them. We must give ourselves in order to understand who we really are. It is through this kind of service that life has meaning. This kind of service is, in truth, the model for leadership that makes a difference. John Wesley believed that our gifts of service would spring naturally from our faith in God.

Robert K. Greenleaf, in his book *Servant Leadership*, says that the servant-leader is servant first; it all begins with the natural feeling that one wants to serve, to make sure that other people's needs are met. The question for a servant-leader, Greenleaf says, is whether those who are served grow as persons and become healthier, wiser, freer, and more autonomous. Are they likely to become servants themselves?

That is a question the ancient Hebrews heard from God, early on in their history. God blessed them with land and descendants and possessions—but at the same time, God made it clear that Israel was being blessed so that it, in turn, would be a blessing to others.

The gift of leadership, the gift of service, is given to people so that they may use this gift to bless others. It is a holy task. It is our heritage from ancient Israel. You and I are blessed to be a blessing to others, and we lead by first serving.

Points of Departure

Δ Everyone must work to live, but the purpose of life is to serve and to show compassion and the will to help others. Only then have we become true human beings.
—Albert Schweitzer

Δ Servant and leader—can these two roles be fused in one real person, in all levels of status or calling? If so, can that person live and be productive in the real world of the present? My sense of the present leads me to say yes to both questions.
—From *Servant Leadership* by Robert K. Greenleaf

Δ Wherever you are, as far as you can, you should bring redemption, redemption from the misery brought into the world. . . . The small amount you are able to do is actually much if it only relieves pain, suffering, and fear from any living being, be it human or any other creature. The preservation of life is the true joy.
—From *Reverence for Life* by Albert Schweitzer

Journaling: Ideas for Written Reflection

How is God calling you this week to lead by being a servant to others? How do you feel when serving others?

Prayers: For the World, for Others, for Myself

LAUGHTER:
Does God Have a Sense of Humor?

Opening Prayer

Laughing God, you created us in your image. Bless now our sense of humor, our laughter, and our joy. Amen.

Scripture Focus

When the Lord restored the fortunes of Zion, we were like those who dream. Then our mouth was filled with laughter, and our tongue with shouts of joy. (Psalm 126:1-2)

Daily Scripture Readings

Sunday	Genesis 18:9-15; 21:1-7
Monday	Luke 15:1-10
Tuesday	Esther 9:18-22
Wednesday	Romans 15:13
Thursday	Ecclesiastes 3:1,4
Friday	Isaiah 55:12-13
Saturday	1 Peter 1:3-9

The Focus for Reflection

Bobby Bowden, head football coach at Florida State University, was asked in an interview if he thought God had a sense of humor.

"Does God have a sense of humor? Yeah, sure. Just turn around and take a look at the guy sitting next to you."

Does God have a sense of humor? Just take a look at an aardvark or an anteater or any one of dozens of nature's creatures with long noses or necks or knees. God does, indeed, have a sense of humor.

It all starts with the Bible, of course. In Genesis 17, God tells Abraham, at the age of one hundred, that he and his ninety-year-old wife Sarah are going to have a baby. In the first version of the story, Abraham bursts out laughing in response to the news. In the next chapter, when the story is retold, it is Sarah who is overcome with laughter.

Faith, sometimes, is laughter and humor and absurdity all wrapped up into one. Isaiah tells the faithful, "With joy you will draw water from the wells of salvation" (Isaiah 12:3). With joy.

In 1964, Norman Cousins was struck by a life-threatening illness. His doctors gave him a one-in-five-hundred chance of recovery. Determined to muster all the resources available to him, Cousins set out on an unconventional road to healing, one that included laughter as part of the treatment. "It worked. I made the joyous discovery that ten minutes of genuine belly laughter had an anesthetic effect and would give me at least two hours of pain-free sleep," he reports in *Anatomy of an Illness.*

Our God laughs well, and invites us to do so, too.

Points of Departure

Δ Wit is not the prerogative of the unjust, and there is truly laughter in holy places.
—From *Saint-Watching* by Phyllis McGinley

Δ Laughter is by definition healthy.
—From *The Summer Before the Dark* by Doris Lessing

Δ Another of his [Thomas à Kempis'] tenets . . . is that all mirth is vain and useless, if not sinful. But why then does the Psalmist so often exhort us to rejoice in the Lord and tell us that it becomes the just to be joyful? I think one could hardly desire a more express text than that in the 68th Psalm: "Let the righteous rejoice, and be glad in the Lord; Let them also be merry and joyful."
—John Wesley

Δ I cannot believe that the inscrutable universe turns on an axis of suffering; surely the strange beauty of the world must somewhere rest on pure joy!
—Louise Bogan

Δ Humour is in fact, a prelude to faith; and laughter is the beginning of prayer.
—From *Discerning the Signs of the Times* by Reinhold Niebuhr

Δ God shines when people laugh.
—From *I Believe in the Resurrection of the Body* by Rubem Alves

Journaling: Ideas for Written Reflection

Treat yourself to some humor this week. Think about it. What makes you happy? What makes you laugh? Are you indulging yourself in enough laughter so that God shines through?

Prayers: For the World, for Others, for Myself

LOVE YOUR MOTHER:
You and the Planet

Opening Prayer

I want to rest. I need to rest and allow the earth to rest. I need to reflect and to rediscover the mystery of your creation, O God. Amen.

Scripture Focus

The earth is the Lord's and all that is in it. (Psalm 24:1)

Daily Scripture Readings

Sunday	Psalm 98
Monday	Luke 12:22-31
Tuesday	Genesis 1:26-2:3
Wednesday	Psalm 104
Thursday	Leviticus 25:1-7
Friday	Deuteronomy 22:6-7
Saturday	Isaiah 11:6-9

The Focus for Reflection

These are the overwhelming facts:

> The earth is losing rain forests at the rate of one football field a second.

> Radioactive fallout from the Chernobyl nuclear reactor explosion made vegetables and meat unfit for consumption in wide parts of Europe.

> There is no "away" when you throw something away.

> One of the world's five to ten million species becomes extinct every day.

There is no doubt about it . . . we have placed the earth in great danger. Surely this is not what God intended when the scriptures say God gave humanity dominion over creation. Surely Adam did not name the creatures of the world so that we might kill them off one species at a time.

But what to do?

Start simply. That is what the Quakers would have you do.

Answer for yourself some of the questions the Quakers ask:

> Am I walking gently on the earth? What are some ways I can live more simply, mindful of how my life affects the earth and its resources?

> Do I honor the life of all living things? Do I seek the holiness that God has placed in these things and the measure of light that God has lent them?

> What actions am I taking to reverse the destruction of the earth's ecosystems and to promote her healing?

> Do I recognize that the preparation for and the conduct of war are among the greatest causes of environmental degradation?

> Does my daily life exemplify and reflect my respect for the oneness of creation and my care for the environment?

> Do I examine and appreciate cultures and communities whose lives are based on close harmony with the natural world?

Start simply. Turn off the faucet while you brush your teeth. Bundle newspapers for recycling. If you're able, use stairs instead of the elevator. Even simple things make a difference.

Love your Mother. Walk gently on the earth.

Points of Departure

Δ We affirm the natural world as God's handiwork and dedicate ourselves to its preservation, enhancement, and faithful use by humankind.
—From *The Book of Discipline of The United Methodist Church,* 1988

Δ A number of years ago I attended a seminar on global issues. . . .

During a question-and-answer period, I expressed my frustration, saying, "Sometimes I feel that all I can do is use smaller-watt bulbs or go back to using the manual can opener." . . .

"What I suggest you do," the speaker said, "is pay particular attention to the news for the next several days and see what issue really grips you. See what angers or saddens or frustrates you. Then formulate a plan and do something *each week* to deal with that issue. For example, if warming of the environment grabs you by the lapels, spend fifteen minutes to half an hour each day just reading about it. Do this until you feel well informed. Then join an organization that deals with the problem, or support it financially."
—From *From the Heart* by Ron DelBene with Mary and Herb Montgomery

Δ The high, the low of all creation, God gives to humankind to use. If this privilege is misused, God's Justice permits creation to punish humanity.
—Hildegard of Bingen

Journaling: Ideas for Written Reflection

In *From the Heart*, Ron DelBene notes that he was advised to spend some time identifying something that was of real importance for him. After that, he was to educate himself and then do something about that issue. Spend some time this week identifying for yourself a particular issue that saddens, angers, or concerns you. In your prayer time, see where that concern takes you.

Prayers: For the World, for Others, for Myself

WINNERS AND LOSERS

Opening Prayer

Help me to remember that you are running the race with me this week, O God. Amen.

Scripture Focus

Let us run with perseverance the race that is set before us. (Hebrews 12:1)

Daily Scripture Focus

Sunday	Hebrews 12:1-2
Monday	Luke 7:44-50
Tuesday	Mark 9:35-37
Wednesday	Matthew 5:1-12
Thursday	Luke 6:37-38
Friday	Psalm 37:1-4
Saturday	Isaiah 55:1

The Focus for Reflection

Judas Iscariot was one of the twelve apostles whom Jesus chose to be with him in ministry. He was the treasurer of the group—obviously important. For a relatively small sum of money, Judas offered to lead some of the temple guard to the place where Jesus could be taken captive without arousing much of a scene.

We call it Maundy Thursday. And so it was done. Jesus was arrested and led away—the first step toward crucifixion.

What reasons did Judas have for bringing about this betrayal? Much is speculated, little is known. Yet, by early morning, it was clear to Judas that he had sinned by betraying an innocent Jesus. Judas repented, sure of his sin, and returned the money he had been paid. Then Judas, sure of his sin, repentant, yet unable to believe that God loved him, went out and hanged himself.

Peter, also one of the twelve, also chosen to be part of Christ's ministry, was the "rock" of faith upon which Jesus proclaimed his church would be built. Peter was confident, sure that he, perhaps more than any other, would stand with Jesus even unto death. Yet on the same night that Judas led the temple guard to Jesus, Peter would deny three different times that he even knew Jesus. Peter would watch what would befall Jesus from a distance, both physically and spiritually.

After the third denial, the cock crowed, and Peter remembered and realized the implications of what he had done. He went out and wept bitterly. Peter the rock could more accurately be called Peter the "pebble."

Judas and Peter, both spiritually devastated by that long, dark night, both sorrowful for their actions, stood before God. In the face of God's forgiveness, one chose life, and the other chose death. Judas separated himself violently, struck out at his being, sapping from his body the very life, the very promise of the call from God.

Peter accepted God's forgiveness, chose life, and sought the comfort and guidance of the other ten chosen. Peter huddled with them in that upper room, windows shuttered, doors closed, seeking safety and understanding.

Judas shut out God's love and forgiveness—judging himself, punishing himself, not able to hear or feel God's peace even unto his death. Peter, even through his fear, his shock, his shame and guilt, was able to accept God's love and forgiveness, to hear and to feel that call of Jesus, "Peace be with you."

Judas was buried in the potter's field. Peter found new courage, new strength in the forgiveness of God. Peter became the dominant leader in the first generation church. Judas repented of his sin, but refused to accept God's forgiveness.

What about you? Are you capable of closing God out, refusing forgiveness, seeking self-punishment? Unlike what Judas believed, God is never through with us. God seeks us even, perhaps especially, in our weakest times, our darkest hours.

Let go and let God. Let go of self-punishment, and let God's peace heal and forgive.

Points of Departure

Δ If you have taken a wrong position on a question and someone bests you in the argument, you are not a loser but a winner, for you are better off than you were before; you have gained more than your opponent has. You have learned something you did not know.
—From *Pieces of Eight* by Sydney J. Harris

Δ My parents were content with me if I tried to do as well as I could what I was able to do. I wasn't compared with others whether they were more gifted than I or less gifted. . . . That seems like sound common sense, sound psychology and sound Christianity.

—From *Confessions of a Parish Priest* by Andrew M. Greeley

Journaling: Ideas for Written Reflection

What do you learn from Judas and from Peter about God's gift of forgiveness? What would you say to Judas about forgiveness? To Peter?

What ways have you used in the past to punish yourself, even though God had forgiven you? How does this affect the way you "run the race which is set before you?"

Prayers: For the World, for Others, for Myself

EMBRACING DOUBT

Opening Prayer
Redeemer God, accept all my doubts. Amen.

Scripture Focus
The steadfast love of the Lord never ceases.
(Lamentations 3:22)

Daily Scripture Readings
Sunday	2 Corinthians 4:7-11
Monday	Lamentations 3:22-25
Tuesday	John 20:24-29
Wednesday	Nahum 1:7
Thursday	John 8:12
Friday	1 Corinthians 13:12
Saturday	Luke 2:41-47

The Focus for Reflection

If you've ever been called a "doubting Thomas" you probably realize the title is not considered a compliment. Whoever used that phrase most likely meant to test you, embarrass you, or get your attention. Maybe they were exasperated with all your questions and simply wanted you to shut up. Or perhaps you yourself called someone else a "doubting Thomas" when their questions outweighed your answers.

"Doubting Thomas." The ultimate put-down. Or is it?

In *The Agony of Christianity*, Miguel de Unamuno defines a faith which has no doubts as a faith which is dead. Many of columnist Sydney J. Harris's writings say that those who have easy answers prove that they don't know much about the scope of the questions they are asking. Isaac Bashevis Singer believed that doubt was an important part of all religion. Robert Browning wrote that the more doubt you had, the stronger your faith.

Faith and doubt are not antagonists, according to Lillian Smith. Instead, she said, they work together side by side to strengthen faith. And Margaret Drabble was convinced that when nothing was sure, it meant anything/everything was possible.

Do you have doubts—about the faith, about life, about yourself? Good for you. As unsettling as those doubts may be, nurture them. Polish them. Refine them. For it is only through doubt that faith and knowledge grow. Never fear the questions . . . only fear those who won't let you ask questions.

Don't forget that, when Jesus as a young boy went into the temple, the Bible says he asked his teachers many questions, and they were amazed.

Amaze yourself. Follow in Jesus' footsteps. Be a doubting Thomas. Track down your questions and doubts, and trust that God is pleased with your keen interest.

Points of Departure

Δ Some years ago, my son studied psychology at the University of Western Ontario. I noticed that one of his text books had yellow pages at the end of every chapter. I discovered that the white pages of the text stated firm conclusions. The yellow pages were much more tentative. They were concerned not so much with giving the right answers as asking the right questions.

Every life should have yellow pages of that sort. Sometimes we try to evade the questions which we find unsettling. They disturb us. But questions are a sign of life and vitality, and every life should have some.

—From *A Lover's Quarrel with the World* by R. Maurice Boyd

Δ Doubt is part of the arsenal of faith. It keeps it fresh and honest. In our daring to argue and in our struggle to understand, the blood begins to flow through a tired and worn-out faith.

—From *Soul Making* by Alan W. Jones

Δ Neither our knowledge of God and his purposes for his creation, nor the discoveries of science are static. I must admit that the scientists are often easier for me to understand than the theologians, for many theologians say, "These are the final answers." Whereas the scientists— correction: the best of them—say, "This is how it appears now. If further evidence is to the contrary, we will see where it leads us."

And of course I'm being unfair to the theologians. The best of them, too, are open to this uncertainty, which is closer to the truth which will set us free than any closed system.

—From *Walking on Water* by Madeleine L'Engle

Journaling: Ideas for Written Reflection

What do you think of the statement "faith and doubt work together side by side"? What questions do you have right now about the faith and about yourself that push you to grow?

Prayers: For the World, for Others, for Myself

THE RISKY BUSINESS OF TRUST

Opening Prayer
Steadfast God, I put my trust in you. Amen.

Scripture Focus
In the Lord God you have an everlasting rock.
(Isaiah 26:4)

Daily Scripture Readings
Sunday	John 10:7-17
Monday	Isaiah 26:1-6
Tuesday	Matthew 6:25-33
Wednesday	Psalm 40:4
Thursday	Exodus 16:13-18
Friday	Psalm 37:3-6
Saturday	Proverbs 3:5-8

The Focus for Reflection

I keep waiting for the time when my late-night television watching will reward me with an advertisement for "the revolutionary, all new Trust-O-Matic that really, really works!"

It would be a device designed to let me know when I can or can't trust someone. Point, shoot, and get a trustworthiness-level reading.

But, if such a machine did exist, I would probably have to worry about battery failure, planned obsolescence, extended warranties, and detection from the "Trust-O-Matic Fuzz Busters" that would really, really work better.

All this puts me right back at square one: How do I know who to trust?

How do you know who to trust? There are no easy answers. The short answer is to be careful, but trust. Figuring out who to trust requires the scriptural admonition to be "wise as serpents and innocent as doves" (Matt. 10:16).

Yet, no matter how careful you may be, your trust antennae will occasionally mislead you. Our emotional makeup as human beings requires us to trust at certain minimum levels or else we may develop mental illness. So trust you must!

How much you trust is a lifelong experiment. Florida State University's head football coach Bobby Bowden says that his plan is a simple one: He trusts people until they show him that they are not trustworthy. Then, he no longer trusts them. Simple . . . but according to Coach Bowden, his simple plan has occasionally caused him emotional pain and financial loss.

Jesus originally called twelve disciples to be a foundational part of his ministry, and yet these same disciples were often more worried about personal greatness than concerned with Jesus' teachings.

At the Last Supper when Jesus predicted his betrayal, each disciple, unsure about what his own role would be, asked Jesus if he was the one that would betray the teacher. Even Jesus, ultimately, found his trust in his disciples broken.

Yet through it all, Jesus placed his trust in God to be with him. This allowed Jesus to continue to place his trust in people, knowing that, ultimately, he was loved by God and he could love others in return, even to the point of betrayal.

Trust. No simple matter. Essential for a healthy mental and spiritual life. Wise as serpents. Innocent as doves. God is with you in your trusting.

Points of Departure

Δ God provided quail and manna in the wilderness (Exod. 16:13-18), and Jesus fed the hungry five thousand out of compassion (Mark 6:34,44). God gives sun and rain to both the evil and the good (Matt. 5:45), and Jesus discourages anxiety about survival by pointing to God's care for the birds and lilies (Matt. 6:25-33). The Ten Commandments provide structure and limits for our life, and Jesus offers guidance for finding stability in his parable of the wise man who built his house on the rock (Matt. 7:24-27). God meets our needs for *survival* and *security* in these and many other ways.
—From *Working Out Your Own Beliefs* by Douglas E. Wingeier

Δ Please don't ever get anxious or worried about me, but don't forget to pray for me—I'm sure you don't! I am so sure of God's guiding hand that I hope I shall always be kept in that certainty. You must never doubt that I'm travelling with gratitude and cheerfulness along

the road where I'm being led. My past life is brim-full of God's goodness, and my sins are covered by the forgiving love of Christ crucified.
—From *Letters and Papers from Prison* by Dietrich Bonhoeffer

Δ And so our good Lord answered to all the questions and doubts which I could raise, saying most comfortingly: I may make all things well, and I can make all things well, and I shall make all things well.
—From *Showings* by Julian of Norwich

Journaling: Ideas for Written Reflection
Using a scale of one through ten, take a measure of your trust level. What's your trust level with God? with friends? with professors and other students? What affects your level of trust in relationships with God and with people?

Prayers: For the World, for Others, for Myself

LET GO AND LET GOD

Opening Prayer

Let me give all things over to you, mighty God. Amen.

Scripture Focus

The Lord has done great things for us. (Psalm 126:3)

Daily Scripture Readings

Sunday	1 Corinthians 15:51-58
Monday	1 John 3:1-3
Tuesday	Deuteronomy 10:12-16
Wednesday	Luke 9:23-25
Thursday	Psalm 71:9
Friday	John 11:25-27
Saturday	Luke 8:22-25

The Focus for Reflection

All my life I've heard the phrase "Let go and let God." I've seen those five words printed on bumper stickers, posted in shop windows, embroidered on pillows, and reprinted on posters.

But it wasn't until a few weeks ago, at a Twelve Step meeting, that I heard the rest of the phrase: "Let go and let God be God."

What a startling revelation! A phrase that had at various times in my life brought comfort or doubt, skepticism or belief, now took on a completely different dimension with these two extra words. I wasn't God. God is God. It wasn't my job to be God—all-wise, all-knowing, mistake-free. It was God's job to be God.

My job was to let go of my need to control everything in my life and to trust that God is in charge—not I.

It was freeing. I felt a weight lifted from my shoulders, and I found myself relaxing in the knowledge that it is God's arms that embrace the world, God's love that empowers me, and God's grace that guides life.

Letting go and letting God be God meant making a decision to turn my life and my will over to the care of God. It meant making a decision to live my life with God's help. It meant I was free to do the best I could, knowing that God accepts me in grace.

Letting God be God frees me to let go of things I can't control, of people who come and go, of each day as it is done.

I still sometimes find it hard to let go. Letting go of dreams, letting go of people, letting go of the past—none of that is easy. But life is a process of that kind of letting go.

That's especially clear this time of year, as the school term threatens to come to a close, as you come to realize that it will soon be time to turn toward summer. Letting go allows you to be moved by God beyond yourself, beyond the present to a deeper understanding of who you are, who others are, who God is.

Let go. It is time. It is safe to let God be God.

Points of Departure

Δ We have mastered the moon and lengthened life but have yet to accomplish consistently the art of letting go. The bird in the hand, no matter how lean, is surety against not knowing. We prolong daylight indefinitely for fear of the ensuing dark. . . . Our death grip chokes what we value most. Some loves will not flower until we let them go.
—From *God-with-Us* by Miriam Therese Winter

Δ To let go does not mean that we give up or that we do not care. Rather, it means that we choose to use our energies in another way, giving them another direction.
—From *Praying Our Goodbyes* by Joyce Rupp

Δ My dear friend, abandon yourself, and you will find me. Give up your will and every title to yourself, and you will always come out ahead, for greater grace will be yours the moment you turn yourself over to me once and for all.
—From *The Imitation of Christ* by Thomas à Kempis

Δ Surrender to God is a highly freeing event. It is like opening the lid of a jar and letting the butterfly wing away freely, or like a person paralyzed for years being able to run and jump and dance again. It is the freedom of a bound Lazarus coming forth from the tomb.
—From *Praying Our Goodbyes* by Joyce Rupp

Journaling: Ideas for Written Reflection

What do you need to surrender to God this week? What are you finding hardest to let go of?

Prayers: For the World, for Others, for Myself

REFLECTING ON THE YEAR:
Looking Backward, Looking Forward

Opening Prayer
God, thank you for traveling with me. Amen.

Scripture Focus
[God] set my feet upon a rock, making my steps secure. (Psalm 40:2)

Daily Scripture Readings
Sunday	Philippians 4:8-9
Monday	Exodus 12:14-17
Tuesday	1 Timothy 4:11-12
Wednesday	Psalm 1:1-3
Thursday	John 20:19-23
Friday	2 Corinthians 4:7-15
Saturday	John 3:8

The Focus for Reflection

Lily Tomlin does a comedy sketch called "Things My Mother Told Me that Later Turned Out Not to Be True." I wonder if she wrote it at the end of her first year in college.

There's a saying my own mother repeated to me often as I was growing up that, sure enough, later did turn out to be true. "God made the road ahead curved so we cannot see what is before us, just around the next bend."

Who could have known last summer where the coming fall and winter and spring would take you? Who could have seen ahead to what these past months would reveal to you about yourself? Who could have guessed at the things your first year in college would teach you? Who could have foreseen the challenges and discoveries your faith encountered this past year?

All the unspeakable goodness and all the unhelpable badness in your life . . . no one—least of all you yourself—could have predicted what this school year would have been like for you.

Take some time to think about what has happened to/for/because of you this year. Celebrate the good stuff and rejoice. Recall the painful stuff and offer it to God for healing. Call to heart the myriad of feelings of the past months and bless them with peace and thanksgiving.

Celebrating, marking, remembering the end of a school year is important work. Like the ancient Greek god Janus, who had two faces—one that looked backward, one that looked forward—we must look to the past and to the future.

As you mark the end of your first year in college, take some time in prayer to look over the past and to look toward the future. The road behind you has had its shortcuts, U-turns, and dead ends, but God has traveled that road with you.

The same is true of the road ahead. It, too, will have its shortcuts, its wild goose chases, and its switchbacks. But God journeys with you on that road, too.

Points of Departure

Δ Celebration is the honoring of that which we hold most dear. Celebration is delighting in that which tells us who we are. Celebration is taking the time to cherish each other. Celebration is returning with open arms and thankful hearts to our Maker.
—From *Why Not Celebrate!* by Sara Wenger Shenk

Δ i have changed
so much
in this world
    i am
constantly amazed
to find
the world has
changed
so little,
    and yet
        i have changed
        so little
           i am
        constantly amazed
        to find that
        the world has
        changed
        at all.
—From "i have changed so much in this world" by Carolyn M. Rodgers

Journaling: Ideas for Written Reflection

Sit quietly for a while and reflect over the past year. Write down your thoughts and feelings. Then spend some time looking ahead, and write about that. How has God been with you?

Prayers: For the World, for Others, for Myself

MOVING ON IN FAITH

Opening Prayer
Guard all my comings and goings, God. Amen.

Scripture Focus
My God in . . . steadfast love will meet me.
(Psalm 59:10)

Daily Scripture Readings
Sunday	Isaiah 42:5-7
Monday	Philippians 4:16-18
Tuesday	Numbers 6:22-27
Wednesday	Deuteronomy 33:12
Thursday	Romans 14:7-9
Friday	Exodus 14:30-15:3
Saturday	Psalm 139:1-18

The Focus for Reflection

At every turn, the Bible says, life links us with the Lord.

And there are so many turns, so many links in a lifetime. Days turn into weeks. Weeks turn into months. Months turn into school terms.

And suddenly, the school year is over, and it is time to move on. Suddenly, it is time to say good-bye to good friends who, just last fall, were strangers to you.

It's time to pack up your dorm room or your apartment or your commuter's survival tools and move on.

We are, like the Israelites and like Jesus, pilgrim people. We are called to go certain places, to do certain things, and then, when those things are finished, to pack up and move on.

Leaving school, leaving your first year in college, is a lot like leaving home was a year ago. Packing up to move on once again requires deciding what to take along and what to leave behind.

You've got all your new knowledge about geology and English and calculus and political science to take with you. You've got memories and friendships to carry along. You've got your experiences in dating and doing your own laundry and making your own decisions to pack up.

As you leave your first year in college behind, you'll take along the value system that you worked so hard to examine and develop throughout that year. And you'll probably have new understandings about who you are and who you want to be that will need to be sorted and packed for the transition to your sophomore year.

There will, of course, be the usual stuff to leave behind—ideas and opinions you've outgrown, excuses that have worn out, faith beliefs that upon examination turned out to be less than true. You may be surprised at what you'll find when you clean out your closet or sweep underneath your bed—there may be some stuff that you'd forgotten you brought with you to college and now discover you no longer need.

Packing up. Moving on. In faith. At every turn, the Bible says, life links us to the Lord.

Points of Departure

△ Whenever it is time for goodbyes, for leaving behind and for moving on, I think of Jesus. I think of how many goodbyes he said, how many farewell tears he wiped away, how many hellos he walked into, how many risks of moving on he accepted.
—From *Praying Our Goodbyes* by Joyce Rupp

△ For me, moving and staying at home, traveling and arriving, are all of a piece. The world is full of homes in which I have lived for a day, a month, a year, or much longer.
—From *Blackberry Winter* by Margaret Mead

△ What then is permanent? What do I have that is mine forever? Of what can it be said, this will not be lost or taken away? My answer is: the promise of God to be with us always. That is the one thing which the brevity and impermanence of life will not take away.
—From *Why Do Mullet Jump?* by Gene Zimmerman

△ For *Sayonara*, literally translated, "Since it must be so," of all the good-byes I have heard is the most beautiful. . . . *Sayonara* says neither too much nor too little. It is a simple acceptance of fact. All understanding of life lies in its limits.
—From *North to the Orient* by Anne Morrow Lindbergh

Journaling: Ideas for Written Reflection

As you pack up to leave school for the summer, make two lists: things you want to take along and things you want to leave behind. How do these lists compare with the ones you made for yourself as you were leaving home last September?

Prayers: For the World, for Others, for Myself

REFLECTING ON THE MONTH

Look back over the past four weeks—the issues, the scriptures, the essays, the excerpts, your journal.

1) Of all the issues and ideas, which touched your life most powerfully? Which still need your time and attention?

2) Which scripture spoke most deeply to your life this month?

3) What reflection, action, or prayer concern do you want to follow up on in the weeks ahead?

Acknowledgments

The publisher gratefully acknowledges permission to reprint the following copyrighted material:

A New Day. Copyright © 1988 by J.B.W. Used by permission of Bantam Books, a division of Bantam Doubleday Dell Publishing Group, Inc.

Elizabeth O'Connor: From *Eighth Day of Creation.* Copyright © 1971 by Elizabeth O'Connor. Used by permission of Word, Inc., Dallas, TX.

Parker J. Palmer: From *To Know As We Are Known.* Copyright © 1983 by Parker J. Palmer. Reprinted by permission of HarperCollins Publishers, Inc.

Jeremy Rifkin: From *Time Wars.* Copyright © 1987 by Jeremy Rifkin. Reprinted by permission of Henry Holt and Company, Inc. and the William Morris Agency.

Carolyn M. Rodgers: "i have changed so much in this world" from *How I Got Ovah* by Carolyn M. Rodgers. Copyright © 1968, 1969, 1970, 1971, 1972, 1973, 1975 by Carolyn M. Rodgers. Used by permission of Doubleday, a division of Bantam Doubleday Dell Publishing Group, Inc.

Joyce Rupp: From *Praying Our Goodbyes.* Copyright © 1985 by Ave Maria Press, Notre Dame, IN 46556. All rights reserved. Used with permission.

Thomas à Kempis: From *The Imitation of Christ.* translated by William Creasy. Copyright © 1989 by Ave Maria Press, Notre Dame, IN 46556. All rights reserved. Used with permission.

Howard Thurman: From "Beginnings" in *With Head and Heart.* Copyright © 1979 by Howard Thurman. Reprinted by permission of Harcourt Brace Jovanovich, Inc.

Paul Tournier: From *Guilt and Grace.* Copyright © 1962 by Hodder & Stoughton, Ltd. Reprinted by permission of HarperCollins Publishers, Inc. and Hodder & Stoughton, Ltd.

The Twelve Steps and Twelve Traditions. Reprinted by permission of Alcoholics Anonymous World Services, Inc.

Phyllis Tyler-Wayman: From "Beauty that Heals." Used by permission of the author.

Walter Wangerin, Jr. From *Ragman and Other Cries of Faith.* Copyright © 1984 by Walter Wangerin, Jr. Reprinted by permission of HarperCollins Publishers, Inc.

Index of Readings

Allen, Paula Gunn, 90
Alves, Rubem, 199
Antrim, Minna, 131
Augustine, Saint, 168
Bach, George R., 179
Beattie, Melody, 131, 155
Bogan, Louise, 199
Bonhoeffer, Dietrich, 51, 116, 126, 183, 215
Bowden, Bobby, 111
Boyd, R. Maurice, 126, 168, 211
Buechner, Frederick, 30, 39, 64, 107, 117, 139, 148, 171
Catherine of Siena, Saint, 139
Coburn, John B., 35, 43, 50, 54
Cousins, Norman, 25, 85, 155
Dahl, Gordon, 107
Day, Dorothy, 103
de Sales, Saint Francis, 122
de Waal, Esther, 54, 99, 138, 147, 156
DelBene, Ron, 39, 203
Dickinson, Emily, 188
Edelstein, Scott, 79
Einstein, Albert, 183
Ettinger, Thomas C., 115, 126
Finley, James, 99
Fowler, Jim, 184
Francis of Assisi, Saint, 131
Fulghum, Robert, 25, 44, 135
Fénelon, François, 54
Gibson, James E., 35
Goldberg, Herb, 179
Goodman, Ellen, 89
Greeley, Andrew M., 208
Greenleaf, Robert K., 195
Hamerton-Kelly, Robert G., 191

Harris, Sydney J., 24, 85, 86, 100, 121, 143, 179, 207
Havel, Václav, 187
Hays, Edward, 51
Herbert, George, 131
Heschel, Abraham Joshua, 30, 69
Hildegard of Bingen, 204
Hillesum, Etty, 43
Holmes, Oliver Wendell, 74
Horace, 90
Jones, W. Paul, 51, 155
Jones, Rufus M., 69
Jones, Alan W., 69, 116, 122, 171, 190, 211
Julian of Norwich, 216
Kalas, J. Ellsworth, 187
Keen, Sam, 184
Kelly, Thomas R., 183
Kempis, Thomas à, 47, 116, 125, 142, 191, 219
Kierkegaard, Søren, 44
King, Martin Luther, Jr., 142
Lawrence, Brother, 159
L'Engle, Madeleine, 43, 55, 211
Lessing, Doris, 199
Lewis, C.S., 35, 163, 171
Lindbergh, Anne Morrow, 30, 136, 227
McGinley, Phyllis, 199
McGinnis, Alan Loy, 103
Mead, Margaret, 227
Merton, Thomas, 30, 70, 90, 107
Miles, Josephine, 80
Muggeridge, Malcolm, 174
Neinast, Helen R., 85, 138
Newton, John, 171
Niebuhr, Reinhold, 80, 199
O'Connor, Elizabeth, 29
Palmer, Parker J., 47, 188
Rifkin, Jeremy, 59, 89
Ripple, Paula, 103

Rodgers, Carolyn M., 223
Rupp, Joyce, 47, 219, 227
Schweitzer, Albert, 195
Shakespeare, William, 163
Shenk, Sara Wenger, 223
Teresa, Mother (of Calcutta), 163
Teresa of Avila, 111
Thurman, Howard, 74, 107, 135
Thérèse of Lisieux, Saint, 46
Tillich, Paul, 175
Tournier, Paul, 103, 179
Tyler-Wayman, Phyllis, 164
Wangerin, Walter Jr., 111, 147
Weil, Simone, 86
Welty, Eudora, 59
Wesley, John, 40, 70, 107, 125, 152, 199
Wiederkehr, Macrina, 152
Wingeier, Douglas E., 63, 215
Winter, Miriam Therese, 219
Wright, Wendy M., 143
Wuellner, Flora Slosson, 51
Yates, Elizabeth, 191
Zimmerman, Gene, 58, 59, 95, 99, 110, 159, 227

Note from the Authors

We would really like to know what you think about this prayer guide. How did you use the reflections? Were there issues you faced during your first year in college that we didn't talk about? What were they?

What did you learn about your spiritual life while you used this book? Did you write any of your own meditations?

We would love to hear your comments, questions, and insights. You can write to us at this address:

What About God?
Upper Room Books
1908 Grand Avenue
Nashville, TN 37202

Helen R. Neinast
Thomas C. Ettinger